'Stephen Cottrell writes about Christ as if He were here now. As if redemption were possible for all of us, as if the void that threatens to engulf us all could be filled by a personal relationship with Christ in the present. He is a compelling writer.'

Russell Brand

'A deeply thoughtful exposition of faith's transformative power, *Dear England* gave me hope, not only for the future of Christianity, but for a changed world too.'

David Lammy MP

'In this gentle and accessible book, the Archbishop of York takes the reader by the hand to explore big questions of faith, meaning and belonging. In doing so he explores with clarity and insight the changes we face, refreshing both those of us for whom our faith has become perhaps jaded and tired, as well as those of no faith at all. At the same time he invites us all to think again about our purpose and belief – and in so doing provides a route map for our increasingly uncertain future.'

Dame Julia Unwin, Chair of Future of Civil Society

'Here's a refreshing, candid, unabashed and, mercifully, jargon-free letter to all of us. The faith that Stephen Cottrell shares in this book is not shrink-wrapped in the usual churchy clingfilm, but unwrapped and open, exposed to current events, to politics, to the 'thousand natural shocks' we all feel in our daily living; and the faith he commends here is all the more robust, and all the more approachable for that exposure. *Dear England* will be helpful not only to the half-attracted, half-repelled enquirers to whom it is addressed, but also to all those believers who would like help in giving an account of the hope that is in them.'

Revd Malcolm Guite, Girton College, Cambridge

DEAR ENGLAND

*Finding Hope, Taking Heart
and Changing the World*

———

STEPHEN COTTRELL

HODDER &
STOUGHTON

First published in Great Britain in 2021 by Hodder & Stoughton
An Hachette UK company

1

A CIP catalogue record for this title is available from the British Library

Hardback ISBN 978 1 529 36095 0
eBook ISBN 978 1 529 36097 4

Typeset in Sabon MT 11/14 pt by
Palimpsest Book Production Limited, Falkirk, Stirlingshire

Printed and bound in Great Britain by Clays Ltd, Elcograf S.p.A.

Hodder & Stoughton policy is to use papers that are natural,
renewable and recyclable products and made from wood grown in
sustainable forests. The logging and manufacturing processes are expected
to conform to the environmental regulations of the country of origin.

Hodder & Stoughton Ltd
Carmelite House
50 Victoria Embankment
London EC4Y 0DZ

www.hodderfaith.com

'I praise you because
You are artist and scientist
in one.'

R. S. THOMAS
Praise[1]

CONTENTS

Part One

FINDING HOPE

CHAPTER ONE

Dear England,

I was recently buying a coffee at Caffè Nero on Paddington Station.

A flat white.

This was a wise decision. The coffee from Caffè Nero is nicer than the coffee from the trolley on the Virgin train.

I was on my way to Cardiff. The keynote speaker at the Church in Wales symposium on evangelism. It was a big gig. I couldn't be late.

The Church in Wales was relying on me.

While the barista prepared my coffee (buying coffee never used to be so complicated, but a flat white seems to me to have got the proportions of coffee to frothy milk about right), a young woman turned to me, looked me up and down, and said, 'What made you become a priest?'

Now this is an interesting question. In fact, it is my standard interview question. I've asked virtually every priest I've appointed in the last fifteen years what they would say if they bumped into an old friend on a railway platform and were asked why they were a Christian and what difference it made to their lives. Now a complete stranger was asking me my interview question. For real. And I didn't have long to answer. I had to get that train.

So I resisted the temptation to ask her in return why she

was asking me. After all, it wasn't my natural aura of holiness that was giving me away. I was dressed as a priest.

I said I had two answers to her question: one, a very short answer; and one, a slightly longer answer.

My first answer, the short answer, is God.

I said to her that I simply believed in God. That, even though I wasn't brought up going to church, somewhere and somehow on the pathway of my life as I had sought to make sense of what it is to be human and what inhabiting this world could mean, I came to reckon that there is a God and that God is the source, the impetus and the precondition of everything. It hadn't been a sudden, thunderbolt conversion, nor did it mean I was unfamiliar with doubt and darkness. It's just that I had tried to make sense of life, and looked for some meaning in life, and had arrived at a point where life, the universe and everything in it made no sense without God.

Moreover, as a Christian, when I said the word 'God', I saw in my heart the person Jesus. Jesus was the person through whom God had a human face and a human heart. Therefore, the God who was in every other respect unknowable and beyond, the source of everything but, by definition, *outside* of everything as well, had come down to earth, so that God could be known. Jesus was God speaking to us in the only language we understand: which is the language of another human life.

That was the short answer!

The slightly longer answer was that I wanted to change the world.

I asked her what she thought and felt when she looked at the world, and I told her what I saw was hurt and confusion. Oh, of course, there were fantastically beautiful, glorious and wonderful things as well. The world is brimming with expectancy and elation. But there is also injustice and horror, and while those persist, joy would always be tempered by caution and concern.

I also told her that I had made a diagnosis. I told her I thought the problem lay in the human heart. I told her that I thought the human race needed a heart transplant. And I told her that, as I saw it, only God could do that.

Why was I a priest? Or for that matter, why am I a Christian? Why am I a follower of Jesus Christ? Why am I writing this letter that thinks it's a book? It is because I believe in God and I want to change the world. But I don't believe in God in quite the same way as I believe the sky is blue and the sun rises in the east. It is much more like I believe that love is real and that Chopin's nocturnes make me cry. Some things are achingly real, but harder to demonstrate, though dig beneath the surface and we all deal in the common currency of love. And I want to change the world – heart by heart. I cry out for the indignities and privations of the world. I long to see change and I thirst for justice. But I begin with the heart, believing that if my heart can change, then the world can change too.

The woman then said to me – and in many respects her words were much more interesting than mine – that when she met people of faith, she found they largely broke down into two categories. For the first group, faith seemed to be their hobby. They went to church – or, for that matter, the synagogue, the mosque, the temple – but it didn't make much difference to the life they led. In most ways their lives were indistinguishable from other people's lives, except for the fact that they went to church on Sunday. The other group – and these are her precise words; they seared themselves into my mind – 'embraced their faith so tightly, it frightened everyone else away'. (Perhaps your experience has been similar.)

'Is there another way?' she asked me.

But at this point, I had to get the train. I couldn't miss it. There wasn't time for the conversation I thought we needed to have. So I just said, yes, there was another way: the way of Jesus Christ. I said that Christians believe that Jesus not only showed us what God is like, but shows us what humanity *could* be like. I told her to go to her local church and she would find it.

But that's what really bothers me. If she did follow my advice and go to her local church, wherever that was, what would she find? Would she find a group of people who are joyfully trying to inhabit this world after the way of Christ? Or would it be a group of Christian hobbyists? Or something worse?

So this is what this book is about. It is a letter to this young woman, for I saw in her something that I see in so much of our culture. She was genuinely seeking for some meaning in her life beyond herself and beyond the things she had already been taught and experienced. She initiated the conversation, not me. Amazingly, she saw in my clerical collar (and hopefully in my demeanour) some representation of a worldview that might just scratch the itch of her spiritual longing.

This book is what I would have said to her if I had had more time. And in a small way it is also a letter to the Church of England (and other churches are welcome to receive it too if they'd like). I want to remind us that our primary vocation is to share this story and to tell people about God and God's vision for the world. There are lots of other things we need to do as well – not least live it out each day – but it has to begin with the story itself: the amazing, inexplicable, challenging and lovely story of what God has done in Jesus Christ to change the course of human history and to win our hearts.

And I've called it *Dear England* because in writing to this woman I am also, if it doesn't sound too presumptuous, trying to write to everyone. The moorings of our culture have slipped from the passage of the Christian way, and other, sometimes malign and confused, currents now sweep us this way and that and leave us not knowing who we are, still less where we are going. This book can't solve all that, but in reading it (and reading it won't take long; it is not a hefty tome) you might see something of God and something of God's purposes for the world.

The very first Christians weren't called Christians, they were called followers of the way. I like that sobriquet. It indicates a pathway to follow rather than a list of things to believe in. In fact, Jesus himself said, 'I am the way.' He is a companion, not a map. Let us see what life looks like if we walk with him.

CHAPTER TWO

I'm writing this because I want to explain to you why I am a Christian and why I'm trying to follow the Christian way.

I know that for many people even the word 'Christian' makes them wince a little. I was like that once. Although I was baptised as a baby, and fortunate to be part of a loving, secure family, I wasn't brought up as a member of the Church. There was belief in my home, but there wasn't church. Not to begin with. As a result, I pretty much adopted the same secular worldview that shapes the lives of most people growing up in England today. God either didn't exist at all: science has disproved that was the vague notion that controlled my thinking. Or else God was an uninterested absentee landlord. Consequently, the word 'Christian' seemed to denote all the uncool out-of-touchness that I was trying to avoid.

Spirituality was something interesting, in the way that religion was not. But I thought spirituality was about deep inner feelings, ecstatic experiences, or about getting in touch with forces and powers outside myself, or else some indefinable 'real me' inside myself.

None of it was formed by what I now know to be the vast, deep, Judeo-Christian tradition that actually shaped the civilisation, laws, culture of the world and the culture I was born into, and that has its own very scandalously specific way of looking at what it means to be human and who God is. Though, having said that, there was a bit of me that always believed in God and had a sense of God – and it is surprising how this is the case for many children. Whether they have been brought up in a faith or not, children still have an inkling of God and are sophisticated enough in this unformed faith to draw a distinction between this inchoate sense of God and their other soon-to-be-discarded beliefs in Father Christmas, Easter bunnies and tooth fairies. They seem to know – as I think I did – that God is different.

Now I am a Christian.

I am someone who has moved from scepticism to faith. I am part of that tradition. It has shaped me afresh.

The temptation for me now is to retreat into a cosy, little Christian sub-culture, cocooned by the safe believing of others and forgetful of the incredulity of those outside the Church. Or I could simply separate faith from the rest of life – this is what happens to many Christians in England today. Friends who are not Christian either do not realise you believe at all, or else you end up trying to win favour ('I'm not really like all those other naff Christians') by gently mocking the faith that actually means so much.

So I am trying another tack. I am trying to explain *why* I became a Christian and *why* being a Christian helps me make sense of life.

And I'm doing it so as to commend the Christian faith to those who don't believe and who don't go to church. I'm trying to convert you, but I'm going to do it by asking you to look at your own experience and the claims of the Christian faith in a fresh light. And if you end up unconverted, I won't think I've failed. This is your decision and no one can make it for you. And since, as we shall come on to, God isn't going to force your hand, I won't try to either. But I do hope you enjoy the ride.

Let's be clear, though: everyone wants a way of living that has meaning and value. There's nothing particularly religious about this. The quest for purpose is part of what it is to be human. (Even the excesses of our own age have not extinguished this noble instinct. And the coronavirus has brought questions of meaning and mortality into sharp focus.)

We instinctively feel that there is a consequence to our lives. Well, this is the beginning of a spiritual search, even if for many people nowadays it has not progressed very far, being so inhibited by a culture that has over-stressed the material and the transient.

I have come to believe that the best way of making sense of life is the Christian way. For the most part I have arrived at this conclusion by reflecting on my own experience of life and looking at the Christian faith from this perspective. Though, of course, before too long you need also to look at the person of Jesus and decide whether what people say about him is true or not. And that is all this letter that has turned into a book sets out to do: to enable you to have a good look.

But because in today's culture even admitting you are a Christian means that you may not be taken seriously (and because I also realise that people who are not Christians may never read this at all – far too uncool – and I want to encourage you if you have got this far), I want to commend the Christian faith in a way that avoids two particular pitfalls.

Usually, people make the case for the Christian faith by appealing either to the trump card of their own particular spiritual experiences – and, authentic or otherwise, you just cannot gainsay that approach – or else they appeal to the authority (and divine inspiration) of Scripture.

I am going to try and avoid this special pleading. I want to state the Christian claims for life in a way that does not depend on fantastic spiritual experience or by always turning to the Bible to prove a point. If you are inside the Christian Church, these things will make sense, but, as I well remember, if you are outside, they just won't wash at all.

This is not to say that I haven't had all sorts of spiritual experiences, which I could tell you about, though I have never had a dramatic conversion experience. Things have happened to me that seem to be the work of God, but that is only the case as I look back and view them from the perspective of faith. I don't expect you to be impressed by them at the moment. That is why I won't be writing about them here. Though I suspect one or two might wriggle their way into the narrative at some point. Apologies in advance.

I have also come to love and cherish the Bible. I read it every day. It is a beautiful and complicated narrative that challenges and inspires me at every turn. But we need to read it carefully and respectfully, understanding how it came into being. The Bible contains different types of truth. You need to be able to distinguish between them.

But I am still a thinking, questing human being; still shaped by the attitudes and conclusions of the twenty-first century. This is inevitable; we cannot help but be people of our own age, so I bring this to my reading of the Bible. However, I read the Bible having arrived at a point where I can say that the most important truth of all, the truth that the stories and narratives in the Bible enshrine, the truth upon which all other truths are contingent, is the truth about the universe, and about humanity, that has been revealed in the life, death and resurrection of Jesus of Nazareth. This is the truth that now shapes my life. It is why I call myself a Christian (though I think I may prefer 'follower of Jesus Christ' if I have to have a label). It is what has made my life more beautiful and more meaningful. But I know that this isn't where you are at the moment. So we will get to the Bible, but only towards the end of the book, and only when we have decided to open it, not because it has the last word on all our questions, but because it offers the *first* word on the new way of looking at life that we are beginning to consider afresh.

The story I am going to tell in this letter, therefore, is of how Christian faith makes sense of life, giving a framework for how we deal with its biggest questions and with the deepest longings of the human heart. And how the values and ideals of the Christian faith that arise from specific beliefs (which are themselves rooted in a particular history) can shape the way we order the world. And by trying to do this without quoting the Bible, at least not to begin with, and without resorting to personal experiences of God, I hope to remove some of the obstacles that could be getting in the way of faith for those who, like me, were brought up in a secular world and have been denied the opportunity to think clearly about the claims of faith.

I want to try and show you that it is *reasonable* to believe. I also want to give you a glimpse of the possibility of the *amazing* God who is known to us through Jesus Christ. And I'm doing it in the form of a letter. Quite a long one!

CHAPTER THREE

I started writing this letter in an England dominated by Brexit. We felt divided among ourselves in a way I have never really known in my lifetime. In fact, like many English people of my generation, I grew up thinking of myself as British, not English. Englishness might even have felt slightly embarrassing. If people asked me where I was from, I think I would say 'Britain', maybe even 'Great Britain', though the 'great' was wearing a little thin. I think I also took Europe for granted, and even felt a little bit European, even though I was always aware that the Channel separated us from what my parents' generation called 'the Continent', a place that was definitely separate from us. The Channel, in this narrative, had saved us on several occasions, one of them within their own living and vividly present memory. But now there was a tunnel underneath it. Now we all had passports that said 'EU' on them. It seemed inevitable that this growing together as one Europe, and maybe even one world, was inevitable.

This was the world I grew up in, and with it a welfare state and a set of ideas about how we belonged together. So, for instance, I spent six years in higher education and it didn't cost either me or my parents a penny. Not only that, but I received a maintenance grant and finished those six years without a penny of debt. I was even allowed to sign on the dole in the long summer vacations. That may have been a generosity too far, but it aptly illustrates how the world has changed.

I simply do not know how much debt my youngest son has accumulated; and he was only at university for three years. But it wasn't just education; it was also a health service, a state pension, child benefit, a whole system of social care, that was rooted in and flowed from a set of ideas that had been forged in the cauldron of the horrors and privations of the Second World War and now emerged in a nation that seemed to believe that everyone mattered and that everyone needed a stake in the future. For a time, and of course to different degrees, all political parties signed up to it. It is referred to as the post-war consensus. What is also interesting to note from a Christian perspective is that it is probably the last really significant contribution to public life that the Church of England has made. William Temple, Archbishop of Canterbury at the time and a brilliant social thinker and theologian, was one of the intellectual drivers behind what became the welfare state.

At the same time, in what I suppose I'm going to have to call mainland Europe, similar ideals were driving nations that had so recently been tearing each other apart to build bonds of economic unity. The European Union may have changed hugely over the years, but it is wise to remember that the main impetus for the creation of its forerunner, the Council of Europe in 1948, was not a common currency, but a common destiny, not the creation of a free trade zone, but peace. This desire for peace was pragmatic as well as principled. As Robert Schuman, the French Foreign Minister, said in 1950 when announcing a plan to pool coal and steel production: solidarity in production would make war between France and Germany 'not merely unthinkable but materially impossible'.

A lot more could be said, but my point is a simple one: what happened in this country in 1945, and what happened in Europe at the same time, was motivated by a vision of what the world could be like if we worked together and if we recognised our common humanity beyond the boundaries of nation and class that had nearly always divided us. And as we shall come on to see, this vision is a profoundly Christian one. It is not actually about the political agenda of any one party (as I've inferred, most political parties at the time, to one degree or another, signed up to it). However, it is not a vision that is self-evidently good or right. It is something that has to be secured, intellectually, emotionally and philosophically. It is always at risk.

So, of course, there were problems. As healthcare, education, life expectancy and a general prosperity rose, so did expectation. And expectation is expensive. So, when I spent my six years in higher education, paid for entirely by the state, only about 14 per cent of the population were taking undergraduate degrees. Nowadays it is more like 40 per cent. That is fantastic. But it is equally very expensive.

We also have very short memories. We quickly forgot what it was like before a welfare state. We quickly forgot what it was like to be at war. We quickly forgot that you need systems and services in place to counter and placate the enmities and prejudices that breed violence.

Peace cannot be taken for granted. Neither can stability. Or welfare. But instead of trying to manage expectations and meet them as far as we were able, we started making exceptions. Banks were bailed out by the public purse following the global economic crisis of 2007 and 2008. But crippling austerity policies for the next decade meant that those who were least able to pay were required to take up the financial slack. Much-needed social services, even things like legal aid, were cut. We ended up in a situation where the gap between rich and poor, which had been closing for decades, started to widen again. Whole communities felt left behind. Even the average age of life expectancy started to go down in some of the poorest and most neglected parts of our country. This gave rise to further suspicions about whose country it was and whose interests were being met. Not only was the idea of a welfare state massively diminished, the only political philosophies that were taking its place seemed rooted in Margaret Thatcher's famous dictum that 'there's no such thing as society'.

Looking again at these words in context, Margaret Thatcher actually had something important to say about families, and partnership between government and people. But that is not how her words are remembered. The saying itself has become a peg upon which a dismantling of ideas that once centred on the common good has accumulated. It reached some sort of nadir when British citizens from the West Indies who had been invited to come and live here in the 1950s as much-needed workers – men and women who had fought alongside us in the war and who proudly carried British passports – were wrongly detained, and some even deported, in the terrible Windrush-generation scandals of 2018. Other fresh waves of mass immigration, particularly from Eastern Europe, bred fear and instability in some communities, usually those who no longer felt they had much of a stake in society or any prospect of the next generation being better off than the current one.

The ideas that had been so unifying and inspiring in 1945 started to seem outdated or irrelevant. They had been chipped away at for such a long time that no one was left to speak up for them. They certainly weren't winning any elections.

It was into these choppy waters that the vote about our membership of the European Union landed. It couldn't help but become a vote about ourselves, not just Europe, and certainly not just the European Union. And different bits of the United Kingdom saw it differently, as did different regions within England. Those who had always felt left behind by a cosmopolitan narrative of being British and European now claimed their English, regional and local birthright. Cities and countryside voted differently. London itself appeared to be a separate country altogether. And those of us who were English started thinking about what that meant, because we were becoming more aware of how the Scots were definitely Scottish, and the Welsh, Welsh.

The vote itself was almost exactly fifty:fifty. But to the winner the spoils. Fifty-two per cent beat 48 per cent, and that was that. The people had decided. Only it didn't feel like that. Especially if you were Scottish.

The debate itself was not edifying. Not on either side. So much of the argument for and against our membership of the European Union seemed either to be scaremongering, or narrowly focused on what might, or might not, be best in terms of our economic interest. There was very little vision about who we might be as a nation or as a world. Little suggestion that human well-being and prosperity might rest on something more than the bottom line on a financial spreadsheet. Neither, at the time, were the electorate rising up and demanding an alternative, so I am not merely blaming the politicians. They were as much caught up in the larger currents of complacency and unimaginative economic conformity as the rest of us, and, as we can now see, it was leading to a crisis.

At least the Scottish independence referendum of 2014, which had narrowly gone the other way, was energised by ideas about nation and belonging. The EU debate quickly degenerated into squabbling about immigration and value for money. These are not unimportant issues. In fact, at the time they were vital: Europe was in the middle of a vast humanitarian crisis brought about by so many people fleeing genocide and warfare in Syria and Iraq. But in or out of the European Union, what was needed was a vision for belonging together, not bartering over how much we can get away with. No such thing was offered.

As we know, the actual leaving of the European Union turned out to be far more complex than even those who had campaigned for it realised. Theresa May was given the unenviable job of delivering a Brexit she didn't vote for herself. There was, at the time, a wisdom in this choice. Someone who voted one way, would deliver in another, and in so doing bring both sides together. It didn't work out that way. Just as when cutting a piece of material, in what you hope will be a straight line and a clean break, it soon starts to fray. The weave of the cloth unravels. The prime minister was held to ransom by the right wing of her own party. An election to break the deadlock failed to deliver and a hung parliament created an uncomfortable political paralysis, like an arm-wrestling match that could never be won. It might have been different if some sort of national government had come together straight away to deliver a way forward that really was about being one nation. But it didn't happen that way. No one was prepared for it. Even those who campaigned to leave had expected to lose.

A campaign for a second referendum gained momentum. Outside parliament, rival versions of what it was to be British and English, and European, exchanged insults. We stopped feeling like the one nation that I had always deep down thought we were.

Then there was a second election and to many people's surprise a big Conservative majority broke the impasse. Suddenly Brexit was being delivered. Some people were delighted. Others were dismayed. At least the arguing was over. Well, at least the first part of it. Boris Johnson, the new prime minister, spoke about one nation. This was encouraging. But there didn't seem to be much substance behind it. Not at first, anyway.

On 31 January 2020 the deed was done. There was no great party. The deal itself – the actual terms on which we were leaving and the vital trade negotiations that would shape our economy and national prosperity for years to come – was still to be negotiated. But, like it or not, we were moving into a new era, and with it a new Englishness was being born and a new way of relating to each other within a 'not quite so United' Kingdom and within a Europe that we still belonged to, but were no longer part of in the same way. Working out what this meant for England, its neglected fringes and heartlands, especially in the north, for the union with Scotland, for the whole of the United Kingdom and especially for the fragile peace in Ireland, and for a new relationship with Europe and the rest of the world seemed to be the big political and philosophical challenge.

How wrong we were. Two days before this, on 29 January, and still not really being reported with any great sense of imminent danger or urgency, the first confirmed cases of Covid-19 were reported in the UK. Two Chinese nationals fell ill at the Staycity Aparthotel in York.

A week later, on 6 February, a British businessman in

Brighton was diagnosed with the virus after catching it in Singapore. He was shortly to be dubbed a 'super spreader', his case being linked to eleven others, five of which were in the UK.

About a month later, on 28 February, the first person to catch the coronavirus in the UK was diagnosed, a man who lived in Surrey, but who had not been abroad. The same day, the first British citizen died from the virus, having caught it on board the *Diamond Princess* cruise ship. The first death in the UK came one week later, on 5 March, when a woman in her seventies was confirmed to have died from the virus. By this point, 100 people in the country had tested positive for Covid-19.

On 24 March, the UK went into lockdown. As I write, with infections from the virus significantly rising again internationally, over forty thousand people have died in this country, thousands and thousands more around the world.

The country that was divided by Brexit is now being united by the fear and anxiety that the coronavirus has spread across the whole world. This dark tragedy, and the terrible sorrows and suffering that have come with it, has forced us to confront ourselves, and especially our mortality. Suddenly, our grasp on life itself feels much less secure. And with this confrontation with realities we had preferred to ignore has come an inevitable examination of all the choices we used to make about how we lived and the values that shaped that living.

What this new unity means – for it is very fragile and could easily break, or worse, become the breeding ground for all sorts of other horrors and extremities – is the other subject of this book. Where could this new sense of belonging together as a nation, and even as a world, lead us and how can it be shaped? What is the vision that can take us forward?

How might we reimagine our common life and serve the common good as we come out of the coronavirus crisis in a similar way that enabled us to be reborn in 1945?

Unlike most other things that will be written on the subject, this book will look at it through the lens of the God in whose image Christians believe we have been made. God is the one who can change hearts and therefore help us change the world. But because, as the author of this book, I have set the bar of my expectations high, I don't want just to write a book for other Christians who already share this worldview to read. Therefore, I am taking you back to Paddington Station, back to that conversation on that day when the world was very different, and when we could talk to each other from less than two metres apart, and where that young woman opened up a conversation that I am now opening up with you, my reader. For it is in this Christian faith that I have found wellsprings of wisdom and delight that can enable all of us to inhabit the world peaceably, and learn again how to tread lightly on an earth we have been plundering for too long.

Dear England, there is a way through the horrors that have been so visited upon us through the coronavirus pandemic. There is a way of being together with each other in our communities and our nations that can reach far beyond the squabbles of the Brexit debate.

It is the way of Jesus Christ. Let me try and explain how I got there and how my heart has been changed.

CHAPTER FOUR

A few years ago, the youth group from Theydon Bois, near Epping, stayed over, pitching their tent in my back garden. I was a stopping-off point on their pilgrimage to St Cedd's beautiful Saxon chapel at Bradwell-on-Sea, a holy place for the East of England.

In the morning before they set off, I gave them breakfast and they said they had some questions for me. One of them was this: is it possible to make a hot dog that is so incredibly, stupendously and unimaginably big that even God wouldn't be able to eat it?

This is an interesting question. And it rests on an all-too-familiar premise that unless dismantled will never get anyone very far when it comes to God.

God is not an object, a created thing, part of the universe like other created things. So the universe is full of stuff. There are the things we can see around us – tables, chairs, mugs, kettles, trees, flowers, sofas, computers, penicillin, raspberries, refrigerators and so on. There is the stuff we cannot see, but know is there, like distant stars and planets and even molecules and atoms *within* all the stuff we can see.

Some of this stuff we think of as natural, such as trees and flowers.

Some of it we know we created, but not from nothing at all. The tables, computers, penicillin and kettles are all made from the so-called 'natural stuff' that we have mined, grown, harvested, examined, analysed, experimented on, ground down and used in ever more ingenious and creative combinations, harnessing energy from steam and coal and gas, and now, thankfully, from wind and sun and wave, so as to be able to enhance our lives on earth and expand the horizons of our knowledge.

We can even create new things that may seem like they have come from nothing at all: like plasma growing in a petri dish; or a cloned animal; or the internet; or splitting the atom. But all of this relies on the stuff within our grasp, the stuff we have taken and broken down and sought to understand and then re-created in so many absorbing and beguiling ways.

With the rapid development of artificial intelligence, it may seem we are even creating life itself and some sort of consciousness. But even this remains contingent upon the stuff we have to hand in one form or another. And although, to the very best of our knowledge, we are the only creatures in the world that have this kind of consciousness (and with it the ability to observe, identify, understand and re-create the world), we are also part of it. We, like all life on earth, have evolved from other forms of life. We may like to think we are the pinnacle of life on earth, and the highest form of life, but we are still part of the stuff that makes up the universe, and not separate from it.

Somewhere far, far away in another galaxy there might be conscious life like us, or even more advanced than us, but as yet we do not know. Our earth might be one of many similar earths dotted around the vast expanse of this limitless universe. Or we might be a single oasis of sentient life in the beautiful but unconscious universe around us.

Either way, when we turn to God, we must concede that whatever we think about God, and even, for the moment, whether we believe in God or not, if there is a God, then God, by definition, must be *outside* of this universe and separate from it, not inside and part of it. Yes, I know the Greek and Roman gods seemed to be both inside *and* outside the universe, but today when people use the word 'god', even if they don't believe in that god, they are speaking about an immense and independent power or force that is outside of what we know and inhabit. Therefore, the answer to the provocatively fascinating question from the Theydon Bois youth group must be *yes* and it must be *no*. It does, in fact, rather depend on what you think God is.

If God is just another created thing inside the universe, just the most powerful thing we can imagine, like the X-Men, Superman and Dumbledore (and every other superhuman something) rolled into one, then, however big and powerful God is, it must be possible to conceive of something bigger, and therefore it would be possible to make a hot dog too big for God to eat.

But if God is *not* just the most powerful thing inside the universe that we can imagine, if God is *outside* the universe (whatever 'outside the universe' means, for now we are using words beyond their limit and trying to imagine that which is unimaginable), then everything *inside* the universe is either irrelevant to God, or in some sense contingent upon God and conceived within the imagination and heart of God. Then, even the hugest hot dog imaginable, bigger even than the universe itself, is still but a bite-sized sausage roll to God.

Where does this take us?

Two things suggest themselves to me.

Thinking of God as being outside the universe does not make it any easier or more logical to believe in God. Neither does it posit with God any particular care for or relationship with the universe. We don't know where the universe comes from. We just know it's here. We are, after all, part of it. Our best current theory of how it started is some sort of 'big bang'. But this is not a physics book. I cannot tell you much more about it, though it is endlessly fascinating to read the accounts of what probably happened in the first milliseconds of the universe's life: matter as dense and tiny as a hazelnut expanding rapidly into all that there is. But we don't know what happened before that moment, or outside it, or even in that very first tiny 'moment within a moment'. It might have been God. It might have been the spark from another parallel universe, one universe bursting into being through the rapidly diminishing black hole of another. We don't know. And even if one day we discover that there was something outside this universe that was its first cause, that still doesn't solve the God question, for, let me reiterate, if there is a God who is more than just the very big, powerful, enormous something somewhere inside the universe, then God is the wrong word to describe it. God, if there is a God, is the source and origin of everything there is, including all the universes and all the stuff there is.

Second, the steady demise of belief in God in most Western cultures has sometimes rested on the absence of proof about God, though as we can now see, that proof could never be available in ways that would brook no objection, because God is not something inside the universe that we are capable of observing and therefore able to prove exists.

But we can't disprove God either. We have to approach the question in another way.

Before coming on to that, though, there is another consequence of God's poor popularity rating that needs to be acknowledged.

When we did believe in God and when we believed that God was the source and origin of everything and when we did, therefore, feel some sort of responsibility to God and relationship with God, and when we even believed that God could guide and shape our life on earth, we tended to have a greater sense of responsibility about how we lived in relation to others and in relation to the world.

Now, I have to put this very carefully. I am not suggesting that it is impossible to have these things without God. Manifestly, this isn't the case. People of no faith at all live lives as good and generous and presentable as those who do. Often better. But when we believed in God there tended to be a greater acceptance that there were moral absolutes: things you should do and things you shouldn't. Much of this has slipped away with the slipping away of God. Though, of course, even the moral certainties that came with God were just as open to abuse by those who would use them for their own immoral ends. So-called holy wars, crusades, colonialism and slavery have all been fuelled by religious and moral certainties. In fact, these very moral certainties provided the justification for what was immoral. So this is never straight-forward. But God did offer a reference point outside of ourselves, and the expectation of being held to account.

We now live in a choice culture, where that choice extends to all realms of life. We see that accelerating in our current internet-driven world. For most of us, there is simply no such thing as an absolute truth: you have your truth, I have mine; as long as we don't hurt each other, what's the problem? Each of us is our own moral judge and jury, and if we don't hurt each other, well what does it matter? Though, actually, the virtual lives that many of us now lead in a world where our online and offline lives blend into each other, and even something as apparently simple as clicking 'buy' on Amazon, raise all sorts of moral questions about where that product came from, how it was produced, stored, dispatched and delivered, and who is profiting from it and by how much. That is before we even begin to consider all the other ways a largely unregulated internet distorts and shapes our lives and our moral choices. Unimaginably horrific material is only ever a couple of clicks away.

How did this come about? That is not easy to answer. But we used to live in a world where God provided some sort of anchor and counterpoint to our own understanding of ourselves. We didn't just think of ourselves as isolated and self-determining individuals. We knew we were part of a created order and we knew that we had some allegiance to God and would benefit from living life the way that God intended. We also had a greater sense of our belonging to each other. Networks of family and community sustained us in very visible ways. Going it alone was a lonely option.

Such a belief in God, and what goes with belief in God as a practical way of inhabiting life, is still the normative experience for most people in the world. Faith is very real in Africa and Asia and much of the Americas. The Christian Church is growing rapidly in Africa and China. Other faiths thrive.

Europe is the exception. Rather troubling for those of us who do believe in God, as societies develop, such as in Europe, there seems to be an inevitability that we decide we don't need God any more, and that God probably doesn't exist anyway. Part of this is the self-sufficiency that the developed world nurtures. But this movement of change in the way we think about ourselves has certainly been accelerated and exacerbated by the darker side of our technological advancement and the huge crises of the twentieth century. There was a time, probably well over a century ago now, when we trusted in progress to the extent that we believed warfare and poverty and maybe even illness would cease. The Somme, Auschwitz and Hiroshima literally blew that away. It also added a further burden of doubt: if this God that we had been believing in was so good and gracious, how were such atrocities allowed to happen?

But there has been another, perhaps even more catastrophic consequence: when we stopped believing we were creatures, part of a created earth that had been created with purpose by God, it accelerated that existing tendency to treat the earth as if it belonged to us. The climate emergency that the world faces at the moment is in part due to a set of attitudes about the earth that we seem incapable of relinquishing. We think the earth is ours. We think we can do with it what we like. Therefore, if we want to fly somewhere for a holiday, we book a flight. If we want strawberries at Christmas, or daffodils in the autumn, we can have them transported from those places in the world where they can be grown at the time of year in question. If we want hamburgers cheaply available on every street corner, well we will just have to chop down that rainforest so that beef cattle can graze. And having watched so many winters leading into so many springs, we think the earth's resources will always renew themselves.

As I write, unimaginably massive forest fires sweep across and devour large expanses of New South Wales in Australia. A lethal concoction of record temperatures, prolonged drought and strong winds have combined to produce an almost uncontrollable blaze. That is, uncontrollable until it rains. But there is no rain in sight. In other parts of the world ice caps melt. Habitats disappear. Remote island communities simply vanish altogether, submerged beneath a rising sea.

Covid-19 has allowed the earth to take a breath. But will we be able to re-set our compass so that it can take another? If not, which low-lying nations will be next? Or whose tinder-dry land will burn?

In the face of this unrelenting change, we tend to place uncritical confidence in our own ingenuity and cleverness. We assume that technological advances will save us where God can't. What we don't seem able to do is change our ways. This, in part, is due to the fact that we don't think of ourselves as being responsible. An absence of belief in God has led to a ridiculous belief in ourselves.

There is, though, another approach.

To understand it you're going to have to bear with me for a few chapters.

Think of it as a little trip to the movies.

When you go to the cinema you have to suspend your disbelief. If you don't, the whole thing will become completely absurd. You have to forget that the people on the screen are actors repeating lines that someone else has written. You have to forget that what you're seeing might be the fifth take, and that they've filmed it from ten different angles. You have to forget that every two or three minutes a director is shouting 'action' and 'cut', that make-up artists and lighting technicians and someone with a sound boom are just off to the left of shot, and that the whole thing is edited, enhanced and dubbed with a soundtrack before you see it in the cinema. Indeed, for the thing to work, you even have to forget you're in a cinema at all.

So what I'm suggesting is this: I'm inviting you to enter the thought world (the big screen) of someone who *does* believe in God. It is incredible – because it can't be proved. But it is also reasonable – it can't be disproved either. It is life's defining influence for those who believe: the thing in life that is most real, shaping the way life is lived and how the world is inhabited.

How does someone reach such a conclusion? Not just that God exists, but that God *matters*. Let's have a look.

CHAPTER FIVE

Stop.

Breathe deeply.

Be still for a moment.

Let the restless and impatient breakers of your mind subside.

Search deep inside yourself for those places where you feel you are most yourself: the things that make you and define you and fill you with delight and awe. Or even the dark and difficult memories – for sometimes it is in the darkness that we have the clearest sense of what the light we crave might actually be like, or at times of pain and loss that we discover just how strong love is.

When was the last time you were stopped in your tracks by a sense of wonder, and what was it that brought you to this abrupt standstill? Was it a poem, or a piece of music, or the perfect and mind-stretching symmetry of a mathematical formula? And how did these things not only fill you with joy but at the same time expand your capacity for joy and wonder and take you to another place where your very humanity seemed to be enlarged and enhanced?

Was it the sky at night or the stillness of water at dawn? Was it the open road stretching as far as you could see, or the East Window at York Minster?

Or what was it like to walk in the darkness, and what did you learn?

Are there experiences and memories that make you feel that you belong in the universe, that you are home and you are safe? Whose company do you long for? And whom do you miss? Whose love and whose presence do you ache for? What was that fragrance that stole into your nostrils from you don't know where, but that instantly transported you back to your grandmother's kitchen and for a moment you felt her arms around you again and felt as though you were home?

Or was it just that your football team won, and even though you know it is faintly ridiculous to be so overjoyed by such a thing (especially when there is so much misery in the world) the fact is that you are? Their travails and successes have somehow woven themselves into your heart and your aspirations. With them you feel some belonging that you've not always found elsewhere.

We are all fantastically different. We all have different experiences and different longings. We all have different ways of feeling that deeply beautiful affirmation of our humanity that comes from an encounter with what we find beautiful and what makes us feel we belong. We will all have endured times of great despair and loneliness when it was the absence of love that made love so very lovely and so very much desired. We will all be moved to wonder by different things.

Some of us will be bored witless by Beethoven's 'Hammerklavier' Sonata, others will weep as we listen, sitting alert and alive on the edge of our chairs holding on to each note and finding in the music vast depths of peace and challenge.

So it is with each other. Love, and all the assorted and associated hurts and passions that go with it, provides us with life's greatest joys and its most terrible sufferings and regrets.

Some of us will remember the nervous passions and the trembling delight of first love when the sound of our beloved's voice, or just the slightest touch of their hand, could conjure joy, when just seeing them and being seen was rapture, when just the memory of presence or the expectation of encounter set our pulse dancing. Others of us will not have had these experiences, or will have been undone or even damaged by them. But for nearly all of us there will be people whose company and presence somehow expand and deepen our own humanity. When we are with them, we feel more ourselves, not less.

Or is there a day that, as you look back over your life, you think: that was the day when I felt most myself, most at ease, most in love, most fulfilled, most full of joy and wonder? Or just a day that was so blessedly beautiful it is the day you would live over again if you had such an option? Or even a day, like the day that a dear loved one died, that was the saddest one imaginable and yet, at the same time, hallowed by unquenchable torrents of tears, a day when we truly knew that though this person had gone, love continued?

Or is there a moment when life just made sense: when your life seemed meaningful, when it had purpose, when what you said and did made a difference? Even if it was a very small thing: something that on its own seemed insignificant but that was somehow woven into a bigger and hugely beautiful tapestry, and you saw yourself as part of it.

I remember one particular moment from my own family life. Our eldest son would have been about two years old at the time. We were living in Chichester and often went for tea in the Bishop Bell Rooms at the Cathedral. In the summer there was a garden where the children could play while the parents drank their coffee. Sitting at the table adjacent to us was a woman who was obviously in some sort of disquiet, but not in a demonstrative way: we were just aware of her solitude and distress. I think I may have even wondered about doing that very un-English thing and reaching out to her. She was carrying some burden of sadness, holding it in, but not so effectively that we were unaware of it. But, of course, I didn't reach out. It's not the polite thing to do and, anyway, how would I know what to say? So we sat in the orbit of her grief, but felt powerless to enter it or change it. We drank our tea. She drank hers.

But Joseph, even aged two, did do something. He was also aware of her sadness. He felt it and he received it, and somehow, however subconsciously and intuitively, he decided to do something about it. He picked a daisy from the lawn and, without saying anything, went up and gave it to her. Watching out of the corner of my eye, I saw her receive the gift of the daisy and thank him, then press the daisy between the pages of the book she had with her. Perhaps she has it there still.

It was a beautiful moment. Joseph doesn't remember it. But in that moment, he was giving this woman something astonishingly precious, something that it is hard to pin down or explain. Yet it is the most obviously wonderful thing there is: one human being, on this occasion a small child, reaching out and doing something to nurse the hurt and assuage the grief of another human being, this time a woman carrying who knows what sadness, and making a connection that spoke more in a single moment than this book, and hundreds of others, will achieve in a thousand pages.

Has someone ever offered you a daisy? Or have you been the bearer of such gifts to others?

Hold on to these experiences of wonder, delight and belonging for a moment. They are the stuff of your humanity; they are the beginning of seeing yourself and your relationship with the world around you differently. In even the hardest of lives there will be moments that we return to, that define who we are and that have shaped our lives for the good.

These feelings are deeply physical – we tend to locate them in our stomach (more about this in a moment) as much as our heart – but they are also what many people will call 'spiritual'. They seem to occupy a place in our consciousness where we are most truly ourselves (so much so that they flood our whole being). In fact, we can't imagine it not being like this.

There seems to be a place within us where love and passion, tenderness, regret, sadness and love (and the dark shadow of loving that is envy, pride and malice) inform and sustain us. It feels like the spark of life itself.

Although the world has many explanations for these feelings, and although the latest science has indeed identified a highway of a million nerves between the brain and the gut in what is called the enteric nervous system (so we really do feel things in our stomach), and despite all the explanations being offered by the decoding of the human genome, we still find ourselves resisting being so unravelled as to be comprehensively explained. And this resistance is more than an anti-intellectual hankering over a simpler and more certain past, where people more readily believed and accepted a view of humanity that clearly identified these feelings and desires within something called the soul.

We human beings seem to instinctively and intuitively believe there is something more to life than what we see around us. This doesn't prove anything, but when we do start to examine these feelings of wonder, delight and belonging, even – perhaps especially – when they are born out of great sadness, and we consider how important they are for our own estimation of what life means and how it might be enhanced and inhabited, we keep bumping up against a conclusion that suggests human life adds up to more than the sum total of our ability to explain ourselves. And every explanation, however intellectually satisfying, ends up unable to satisfactorily explain those feelings with which we began: holding a child's hand; a nocturne by Chopin; a babbling brook; a walk in the mountains; an offered daisy; or a lover's kiss. It's not that the explanations aren't true, it just seems as if there could be another truth that is outside of these truths. A truth that does not neuter or smother the rational truth, but is not dependent upon it either. The truth that is the same sort of truth as the truth about God: something that is intimately connected with, and yet at the same time independent from, the truth of this feeling and this emotion and this longing.

In other words, even if many of us are not actually hankering after an explanation for the so-called spiritual reality that we seem to believe in and still experience as a vitally important thing about ourselves, we do want to find out how life can be more meaningful, more joyful, more hopeful, and how we can have a greater sense of belonging within it. These are the spiritual but not religious children of twenty-first-century Britain, such as the young woman I met on Paddington Station who wants to know about God and how someone might so believe in God as to make God the reference point for everything.

CHAPTER SIX

Surveys consistently show that a great many people in Britain still believe in God (though who or what God might be is not clear) and still pray regularly. Meditation and mindfulness grow in popularity and relevance. Alongside this there is a veritable smorgasbord of emerging and growing belief in all sorts of other things to bring spiritual sustenance, value and meaning. Far from being on the wane in a supposedly rational and scientific age, the search for spiritual reality is actually on the increase, particularly among the young. I mention these other beliefs in as neutral a way as I can. They are evidence of the very thing that I presume the young woman at Paddington Station had been exploring. She wasn't approaching the Christian story from a complete vacuum. She probably knew something about it from school, or possibly even church. She had obviously been looking at other religions as well, and possibly all sorts of so-called alternative spiritualities.

However, what I am arguing here is that even if you are *not* one of those people who looks for meaning and purpose in your life through that growing *pot pourri* of so-called new age spiritualities, you have a spiritual dimension to life (even if you don't use the word) because your experiences of love, wonder, joy, fulfilment, sadness and, yes, even the darker register of these feelings, such as envy, malice, greed and lust, crave an explanation that is more than all the other good and helpful explanations that the rest of the world in all its undoubted cleverness and wisdom provides. It is these things – love, awe, joy and fulfilment, but especially love and our experience of being loved and sensing wonder – that define and delight us. They are a starting point for believing in God. They are 'spiritual' in a way of understanding that slippery word that is often overlooked. So, hold on tight, this definition of spiritual isn't perhaps what you're expecting, but it will begin to get you into the Christian way of looking at God and inhabiting the universe.

Spiritual for me (and for the Christian faith) does not mean awareness of a realm that is separate from us and might be accessed if we just had the right formula. Spiritual is not separate from physical (or from mental or emotional for that matter). Spiritual is that which is within us that binds up the whole, a way of understanding ourselves, where we come from and who we are and where we are going, that is directly related to the God who made us and is the source of our being. It is our route in and back to God. It does not supersede or cancel out all the other things we know about ourselves – our scientific and psychological understanding still holds good and still has much to teach us – but it connects them together with that inexplicable something that is never quite satisfied by all the other explanations. How could it? For in this movie that you are watching at the moment, God is real. Spirituality is the way we understand and access God. It is the gathering together and the summit of all that we are and all that we know. It is not a separate realm, but the coming together and the communion between us and God. And love, our experience of love and even the emptiness we experience when love is absent, is the strongest evidence of all.

So my thesis is simple: the Jewish/Christian claim that

human beings are made in the image of God, although impossible to prove in any way that would close down all discussion, is, for those of us who do believe it, evidenced in the raw material of our humanity, especially those feelings and passions that are to do with love and wonder. It is these things that make us most distinctly human. It is these things that are the connection with God.

Human beings are made – intended – for relationship with God. That connection that we sense, however inchoately, is actually an echo of the deepest truth about who we are.

This declaration that human beings are made in the image of God can be found right at the very beginning of the Hebrew Scriptures (what we Christians call the Bible). God creates humankind in 'our image, in our likeness'.[1] This does not mean that God looks like us, but it could mean that the feelings and thoughts, not least our own innate ability to stand outside as well as inside ourselves, have their origin in God. We, as it were, reflect back to God the consciousness and creativity out of which the universe was created.

Well, that statement needs some unpacking. Park it for a moment. Just focus on our own consciousness, and in a jiffy we will come on to our creativity and our sociability, the way we form ourselves into communities of friendship and family, and let them lead us back to God. But consciousness itself is a good place to go next.

Although we now know that other creatures possess the neurological substrates that generate what we call consciousness, as far as we are able to know we are the only creatures in the universe who possess such developed consciousness that enables us not only to stand outside of ourselves and observe ourselves, but also to make moral and aesthetic judgements about ourselves and the life we experience around us, even to the extent that we seem to break free from mere instinct and act in ways that may be detrimental to ourselves in order to serve a greater good. Actually, it is reassuring to know that the raw materials of this consciousness that has so developed in human beings are also shared with other animals. For people of faith it shows how the whole created universe is created by a God who gives to the universe the very things that are of the nature of God. In fact, the more cosmology reveals of the nature and origin of the universe, and of the place and origin of conscious life within it, the more extraordinary seem the coincidences that have come together to make this planet a fertile oasis within what may well be the barren emptiness of everything else. Of course, we can't know this for sure, nor does it really matter for our purposes here whether there is other conscious life in the universe or not. But it is interesting to note that the more we discover of the phenomenon of life, the more we are amazed by our own fragile brilliance. We do not conclude there must be plenty more of it around: we are dumbfounded we exist at all.

So, for instance, let's consider for a moment the amazing coincidences that have made this universe in which we dwell optimal for the emergence of life. Cosmologists tell us that if the distribution of gases in the universe from the Big Bang onwards had been slightly different:

> or the temperature slightly hotter or colder; or if the total mass of the universe had been slightly smaller or greater; or if there had been a minute reduction of the neutron mass; or if the force of gravity had been slightly weaker; or the force of electromagnetism slightly stronger then the formation of the universe, galaxies, this planet . . . you and I could not have happened.[2]

Cosmologists, of course, do not agree that all these coincidences are down to God. Though many people are surprised by how many do! But even Francis Crick, an atheist famous for his work with James Watson in proposing the structure of DNA, once said: 'An honest man armed with all the knowledge that is available to us now could only state that in some sense the origin of life appears at the moment to be almost a miracle.'[3] What they all agree on is that one of the main reasons that conscious life has emerged on earth – though even this is dependent upon another astonishing set of coincidences that we ourselves are in danger of imperilling at the moment – is the remarkable stability of the climate, and it is foolish to simply exclude the possibility of God from this debate. And, of course, Christian cosmologists – not least people like the Belgian Catholic priest and professor of physics at the Catholic University of Louvain, Georges Lemaître, the originator of the Big Bang theory – say a lot more.

But what everyone agrees on – how could it be otherwise? – is this: conscious life does exist. Here am I communicating these thoughts to you through the miracle of language. And there you are, reading this book, and processing what I am saying, and – in due course – making your mind up about whether these ideas make sense to you, and whether they might even change the way you live your life.

Alone among the creatures of this world we seem to be able to live life beyond instinct: we are able to gauge and shape the life we have, and we are able to reflect purposively on life. We make and understand moral choices. We are able to make decisions that are in our best interests. But we can also make decisions that are in the best interests of everyone. And far more surprising, we sometimes make decisions that are in the best interests of others, but may not benefit us. We understand all this – often intuitively. And we make choices about it.

This consciousness and our desire to make sense of life have spawned an astonishing and bewilderingly varied creativity, leading us in directions that have been beautiful and liberating, but also, sometimes, unspeakably evil. As we consider human achievement – whether it is the poetry of Shakespeare or Sylvia Plath, the songs of Van Morrison, the jazz of New Orleans or Beethoven's final string quartets, Monet's water-lilies, Rothko's expanses of gravid colour or Jenny Saville's cinematographic vistas of human flesh, the triumphs of modern medicine, the declaration of human rights or the wonders of the internet, we find our appreciation of ourselves expanded. But we also shudder in horror at the devastation wrought by the atomic bombs on Hiroshima and Nagasaki, bright, white incinerating death falling out of the sky, killing thousands in an instant. Or the methodical, carefully planned and skilfully executed genocide of the death camps of Auschwitz and Belsen, names that are carved into human memory and chill the blood. Or else we look into the future wondering, apparently helpless, what genetic modification of plants, the production of human organs in pigs, the farming of embryos, the rise of artificial intelligence, or just the skilful way that Amazon and Facebook harvest our data, will mean for our children?

We are terribly clever. So terrible in our cleverness that you may decide that our appalling cruelty is sufficient evidence to dismiss the notion that we are created by a loving God, let alone in God's image. This might be the point where you stop reading this book altogether. But, if you bear with me for a few more pages or, as it were, sit in the cinema just a little longer, what I'm suggesting is that to be made in the image of God is to be made in the image of the one who has made this universe, and has made it with a terrible freedom, which is itself the necessary precondition for creativity and love. It wasn't just coincidences for the sake of coincidence. Neither is it merely a set of coincidences. There is a purpose. The universe possesses this terrible freedom *because* it has been made out of love, and because it is destined for love.

This incredible declaration is, above everything else, the most important thing that Christians believe about God. The Christian belief is that God *is* love and that what God desires is love.

We don't just say God is loving. Nor just that God loves. We say God *is* love; and when we say this we are not merely describing God's actions, but describing God's very nature. And because we are talking about real, fragile, self-giving love – the same love that we experience in our daily lives – we can also recognise that two of the hallmarks of genuine love, hallmarks that define love's very nature and brook no argument, are creativity and freedom.

It's important to note that these are not religious ideas. Reflect simply on your own human experience. When we are in love, that love is creative, whether in the blossoming and realisation of ourselves – for we feel more fully ourselves when we are in relationship with one we love – or else, quite literally, in the wonderful creativity of reproduction. Love, we conclude, is that thing upon which no price can be set or met. As a beautiful poem in the Bible puts it, words that are sometimes read at a wedding service: 'Many waters cannot quench love, neither can floods drown it. If one offered for love all the wealth of one's house, it would be utterly scorned.'[4]

But even if you're not married and not in any sort of relationship, never have been, and never want to be, love is real and love is creative, and this joyful creativity, this desire for communion, to receive and to be received, is, Christians believe, part of the very nature of God. It finds form and expression in myriad different ways. Human relationships are just one of them. And let's remember there are many different kinds of human relationship, not least the love of friendship. There is also the love that is poured into the work that we do, in the way we seek to make sense of and even re-create the world around us, and in the commitments we make. We may well say we love our family. But we also say we love our work, we love our community, we love the world. We also love certain pieces of music, or places, or books. This is still love. These things speak to us and change us and are themselves the product of the love and commitments of others.

Then there are the ideas and ideals that we love and give our wholehearted commitment to, and may even die for. This love – the love that lays itself down for another person or for a cause – is an astonishing thing. Like all love it can and has been abused and distorted and turned in on itself. But it has also shown us the greatest love of all. For love that is only confined to one other person is actually not the highest ideal of love. Moreover, romantic ideas about such love can diminish love's harder and more fulfilling aspirations.

Love is always striving for greater community and, as we shall see later on, greater justice. The ideas that we love about the kind of world we want to inhabit and how we might build such a world, and the sacrifices we might be prepared to make to see such love lived out, are perhaps the greatest sign of the God who *is* love and made us out of love.

This leads us from consciousness to creativity to

community. Perhaps we might even dare to say that God cannot help but be creative. God's creativity, even in the creation of the universe, is the overflow of God's love.

Therefore, a Christian answer to the question of the origin of the universe is that the Big Bang with which the universe began, the tiniest hazelnut of matter expanding rapidly and inventively into all that is, was the profoundly beautiful consequence of creative loving. Just as in the splitting of the atom we discovered that matter transforms into expanding energy, so the pure energy of loving within the Godhead itself, within the very being of God, splits and overflows into expanding matter. Within this outpouring of created love was the cherished possibility (though not the certainty) that a creature could evolve and emerge that would be able to reciprocate that love and strive for love in the whole ordering of the world. That again is the nature of love. It is given in absolute freedom, looking for no reward other than the satisfaction of loving. In fact, it is unable to do anything other than love (you cannot by an act of will stop or start the business of love), but it longs for the love to be returned and to be lived out in all the networks of relationship and community that make up the community of the global, human family. Therefore, the character of the universe is the character of unconditional – and therefore completely free – loving. That is also the character of humanity, which, it turns out, is also the thumbprint of the creator God who made the universe out of love.

We are made in the image of God. Therefore, we have this tremendous capacity to love and to create. We seem to have a vision inside us of a world ordered by love. And a longing to use our best gifts of creativity and love to make that vision real.

CHAPTER SEVEN

So let's complicate matters further, and add another layer of mystery and delight.

When Christians speak about God their most profoundly important (and, at first, inexplicable) language concerns a description of God as community: the one who is known to us as Father, Son and Holy Spirit.

Many Christians find this is a difficult notion, and we will return to it. It is hugely important. But for the moment just hold the idea in your head that when Christians speak about God they are also speaking about community. Moreover, although the word 'father' is used, God has no gender. Christianity has had a long and difficult entanglement with patriarchy, but in the Scriptures themselves and in the Christian tradition there has always been a growing under-standing that God is somehow both above gender and includes all identities. God, as many ancient Christian writers have testified,[1] is father and mother, but more besides in the aston-ishing ideas of community that the relational language of Father, Son and Spirit point towards. Within God, therefore, there is a giving and receiving of love within a community of persons. It is from this giving and receiving of love that creation flows, for this is how it must be with love.

How do we know?

Well, because we know about love. We know that love is always creative, and that it is always looking to form community. And we know that flowing from that community is more love and more community.

We also know that we are social beings. We cannot and do not exist on our own. We are at our best when we form community with each other. More than that, we find ourselves and discover ourselves in relation to each other.

Like God, the community of the Father, Son and Holy Spirit, we are at our best and our most creative and most fully ourselves when we discover who we are in community with others: in relationships; in family groups; and as interdependent communities. We, too, give and receive and create out of these networks of loving relationships. And even though certain philosophies and ways of looking at the world have tried to persuade us that we are best understood as self-determining individuals, we actually find the compass of our inner selves returns to look for others, and it is in relationship with them that we find we are most ourselves.

This is the tremendous giving and receiving of love that is the way we reflect and imitate (without necessarily realising it) the God who made us.

Again, we know this, not because we've read it somewhere, or been persuaded towards a certain view: it is our experience. We know that love is not a finite resource. You can give it all away completely and still have every bit of it left to give again. We know that there isn't a limited supply of love. You don't need to ration it. You don't need to give just a small slice of love away so that there will be enough to go round. I can give you all of my love, the whole caboodle, and still have all of it left to give to another. And another. And another. Love replenishes itself by being given away. So God is constantly giving and receiving and overflowing, because God is love.

But because it is love, and because in order for it to be love it is also free, the creation that is made out of love exhibits the same freedom, and with it the same dangers, temptations, snares and severities. Such is the nature of love.

If my love was in any way coerced or manipulated, it is not that what I was offering was 'not quite love' or something 'slightly less than love'. It would not be love at all.

Here is the overwhelmingly important point about love and about God and about faith that we have to get our head round before going any further: *for it to be love it has to be free*. Take away just a tiny bit of the freedom and you take away all the love. So God makes the world with its terrible, beautiful freedom, because that is the only way for it to be love. Therefore, it has to include the freedom that we may never understand who we are or why we're here. It has to include the freedom that we may end up beguiled by all the other truths that anticipate and foreshadow the truth about God, and in the end, through the terrible cleverness of our freedom, may end up replacing God as well.

Therefore, whenever we experience love – whenever we clasp the hands of our beloved, feel the thrill of being welcomed home by child or partner – whenever we realise that there are some things we would die for (though they are more likely to be people than ideas), we are experiencing the echo of the creator God who made us out of this same substance: love.

Free and creative loving permeates our every cell. It is not just a secret pool within us that we used to call the soul, though it still often feels this way and we will still use the language of heart and soul as the most ready way of defining what we feel. But it is more than this. It is the fingerprint of the one who made us.

And because this love is the genuine article of free love, God delights in us just because we are. God shares the thrill of our passions, our homecomings and our sacrifices. God weeps with us in our sadness; God cries out in dismay at our betrayals. And even if we lived all our lives not knowing God and not returning God's love, God would not love us any less. Such is the nature of love: it longs to be returned, but it will carry on loving whether it is returned or not.

If what I am saying is true, then there is nothing we can do to stop God loving us, and nothing God will do to force us to love in return. Therefore, I'm not merely suggesting that there is something missing in your life if you don't acknowledge God. I'm not saying there is some sort of God-shaped hole inside you and you will always feel a little bit empty until it is filled. God has already given the world its freedom and its creativity, therefore you are already the person God created you to be. The possibility of you, of cells combining into life to form your particular, one-off arrangement of the human pattern, was always there from the first moment of creation. Acknowledging God will not change you in this sense. It is not a matter of understanding what you *are*, so much as understanding what you are *for*: that is the key to seeing how Christian faith gives purpose and meaning to life. You are made for community with God. Everything you are and everything you have is a gift from God. Everything you are and everything you can be will find its fulfilment in God.

A good analogy (though all analogies are woefully incomplete) would be a key and a lock. A key without a lock is complete in itself. It cannot be a better key. There is not any part of the key missing. It is just that until it is placed in the lock and turned, it never fulfils what it was created to achieve.

You can therefore be happy without God. But you will

never discover the true purpose of your life. Discovering this purpose may not make you happier. In fact, discovering purpose always leads to challenge and often to adversity. Nevertheless, there is a purpose.

God created us to love: to love ourselves properly, to love each other and to love God. This is our calling. (This by the way was what Jesus said when, trying to catch him out, one of the scribes asked him which of the commandments was the greatest. Jesus replied: 'The first is, "Hear, O Israel: the Lord our God, the Lord is one; you shall love the Lord your God with all your heart, and with all your soul, and with all your mind, and with all your strength." The second is this, "You shall love your neighbour as yourself." There is no other commandment greater than these.')[2]

As we have already noted, all human beings, even though we pervert and abuse it, still reckon love to be the most important thing about life and still long for a meaning and purpose to life that makes sense of love. But if we fail to love God, we are in danger of missing the purpose of our lives. However, when we do begin to live in the fullness of this loving, we discover a true purpose. We give our lives and our love to God and – because this is the nature of love – it is given back to us enhanced and magnified.

And the fact of the matter is that most people don't feel happy. We live in a society of increasing stress, breakdown and disappointment. The coronavirus pandemic has only increased our anxiety, put greater pressure on our leaders and services, and left many of us poorer and more frightened for the future.

For many people there is little or no purpose to life save getting by. Even the notion of fulfilment is only made possible by comparative wealth. Most human beings in most of the world spend each day just trying to get through the day. Other concerns are a luxury they cannot afford.

In our own society, beguiled and seduced by the alluring promises of a material and consumer culture, wealth has become the much-longed-for and highly desirable thing that we strive after. Many people still hope for a win on the Lottery. This would indeed bring great material benefit, but the solution offered by this vain hope is just a very large symptom of what is causing the hurt in the first place. It is another sign of the loss of community, of finding happiness at the expense of others rather than in solidarity with them and for common purpose. We don't so much want to change the world as to become rich enough to escape into another one.

But, of course, most of us don't win. Most of us just go on from day to day feeling frustration at the transience of life, confused and confounded by failed loving and broken relationships, raking regretfully over a past of lost opportunities and fearful of a diminishing future. Life slips through our fingers, and we settle for compromise, resigned to the loss of any hope we may have had, refining our well-honed cynicism for anyone with an alternative vision and grimly awaiting the unwelcome finality of death.

This is the reality of so many lives at the beginning of the twenty-first century. I said earlier, it was the ravages of the last century that have blown all optimism away. But 9/11, the Iraq war, the all-too-numerous genocides of this century, the internal disagreements and alternative narratives about what it means even to inhabit this island, which Brexit brought to the boil, and then the utter misery and fear of Covid-19, have hammered away at the human spirit, and left us even more inclined to look for individual ways of surviving and finding happiness.

All of this can be changed. And that change begins with an honest recognition of who we are – individual, social and creative beings made in the image of the creator God – and of the purpose our lives possess when we live life in community as God intends and desires.

So if all this is true, as I said in my simple answer 'God' to the young woman on Paddington Station, why doesn't God make it a bit easier? Why isn't God actually known to us in a clearer, more tangible way? Why does all the evidence of disease, despair, dying and decaying seem to speak against this optimistic vision?

Yes, there is a love inside me and, yes, the other explanations don't quite satisfy, but I need a little more than fine words. If God really is the origin and the destiny of all life, shouldn't God communicate it with a little more clarity?

And the Christian answer is, God has.

This was the second thing I said to the woman at Paddington. God has communicated love and his purpose with absolute clarity. But this was not an easy thing to do. For the God who *is* love is therefore constrained *by* love, and in wanting nothing other *than* love has to work and communicate within love's constraints (as we do, too: we cannot force anyone to love us). Therefore, God has, if the religious people reading this book will forgive me for a moment, a problem. How do you communicate both the absolute, unconditional fullness of love and at the same time – because love is seeking love – safeguard our freedom to choose how we respond? As we have already noted, if love is to be love, it has to be free. Therefore, if just a little bit of the freedom is lost or compromised, then love itself becomes impossible.

So, conceivably, God could intervene at any given moment. Right now, as you read this book. Or outside Caffè Nero at

Paddington Station. God could come down in a fiery and overwhelmingly persuasive, decisive and irrefutable show of divine and almighty power, and we would be left with no choice but to conclude: yes, there is a God. We would believe. We would probably even obey and conform. It would be foolish and self-defeating not to. But it wouldn't be love.

So God chooses another way: a way of painful and inevitable ambiguity; the way of fragile and self-emptying love; a way that safeguards our freedom and makes love possible. And so we turn to the strange story of Jesus of Nazareth and the incredible claims that Christians make about him. For Christians believe that in Jesus, God shows us what being human is supposed to look like and deals with all the things that separate us from God and from each other. Christians believe that their faith rests not on a cleverly worked-out theory about God and the universe, but on a series of events in human history: the life, death and resurrection of Jesus Christ.

Part Two

TAKING HEART

CHAPTER EIGHT

'In the sixth month the angel Gabriel was sent by God to a town in Galilee called Nazareth, to a virgin engaged to a man whose name was Joseph, of the house of David. The virgin's name was Mary. And he came to her and said, "Greetings, favoured one! The Lord is with you."'[1]

There you are – I told you there would be the odd quote from the Bible. I slipped one or two into the previous chapters, but they didn't really change the way the argument was going. These ones do. These very famous words come from the first chapter of Luke's Gospel (one of four accounts of the life, death and resurrection of Jesus). It's where the story of Jesus usually begins: his birth in Bethlehem. You know, the shepherds, the angels, the wise men, all of that. It's the one bit of the Bible that most people still know. Nativity plays and Christmas carols are still hugely popular, even if many of us attending don't quite know why.

But I want to start somewhere else. Not with the birth of Jesus, not even the death of Jesus. Nor the resurrection, but with some words *about* Jesus – sorry, another little quote from the Bible – that were written by just about his most famous follower apart from those who actually knew him in his earthly life: a man called Paul, who had been an educated and zealous persecutor of the infant Christian Church, but became one of its greatest witnesses and advocates.

Written under house arrest in Rome to one of the many

little churches that had, like seedlings after spring rain, sprung up all over the known world in a remarkably short space of time, Paul said of Jesus: '[He] is the image of the invisible God.'[2]

These words were probably written between the years AD 60 and 62. That is about thirty years after the events that Christians remember as the death and resurrection of Jesus, though some scholars date the words even earlier, thinking Paul might be quoting the words of a very early Christian hymn. This, of course, doesn't prove that Jesus is the image of the invisible God. But it does show that at a very early stage in the development of Christian thinking, his followers were reaching some remarkable conclusions about him.

And Paul is writing while he awaits trial in Rome. He too has been arrested because his faith in Jesus is stirring up the world. The Christian faith is spreading. Its radical ideas about how we belong to each other and how we have access to God confront and threaten the religious and political norms of empire and religion. Moreover, because he had been a persecutor of the Church, Paul has particularly antagonised the leaders of the Jewish faith he had so recently supported.

Jesus shows us what God is like, says Paul. 'He is the image of the invisible God.' Then, a little later on in the same letter, he writes: 'In him the fullness of God was pleased to dwell.'[3]

These are incredible things to say about another human being. But they are the things upon which the Christian faith is built. As the first Christians reflect on their experience of Jesus, these are the conclusions they start to come to.

During his lifetime on earth, Jesus' identity was largely unknown and concealed. As I suggested at the end of the last chapter, he was, after all, communicating God's very self in and through a human life. So if you do ever get round to reading the accounts of Jesus' life in the Gospels you will quickly note that those who follow him don't seem to know who he is. They have hopes of him, but those hopes are dashed. He is neither the religious Saviour nor the political leader they were craving. There are moments of incredible recognition. But there is mainly projection. Jesus is hugely attractive. His presence makes a difference. But people, even his closest followers, don't know who he is. Moreover, his insistence on keeping quiet about himself when he is given an opportunity to explain himself only makes those same followers hugely fearful. In the end, nearly all of them abandon him.

However, as those same followers, now somehow turned around and transformed by their experience of Jesus *after* he had died, reflected on who he is – not just his teaching, but primarily who he was and what he did, and most significantly of all, upon the meaning of his dying and rising (we'll come on to that soon) – they concluded that somehow, amazingly and inexplicably, God was in Jesus. And the only words they could find that would adequately express this conclusion was that somehow – also amazing, also inexplicable – Jesus was the image of God.

Now, I'm not expecting you to necessarily agree with this at the moment, but it is important that you understand that this is what Christians believe about Jesus and believe about God. And it is what was believed from a very early point in the development of Christian thought. In fact, there is no Christian thought without this affirmation.

We are, therefore, not just saying that Jesus is a very good person. Nor just a very wise person. Nor only a brilliant person. We are saying all those things, but we are also saying much more.

We are not saying that Jesus was a great and wonderful prophet, like other great and wonderful prophets. We are not saying that Jesus was so in tune with God that what he said and did was just the closest to God that any human being could possibly get.

We are saying that Jesus *is* God. That Jesus is God come down to earth. Or, in Paul's words: 'the image of the invisible God'. The God whom we have been speaking about throughout this book becomes, in Jesus, a human person, living and breathing and eating, and, yes, all the other things that go with being human. The one through whom the world was made has now entered that very creation to know it first-hand *from the experience of being created.*

Therefore, Christians believe that just about everything we know about God has been shown to us in and through Jesus. Or to put it another way: we don't know anything about God that we don't see in Jesus. Therefore, if we want to know what God is like, we look at Jesus. And if someone suggests something about God that is contrary to what we see in Jesus, then we are fairly confident that they are more likely to be talking about themselves or their own projections of what they would like God to be, rather than the God who is known to us in Jesus.

Incidentally, since we believe there can only be one God, we are also very open to the truths and insights about God that we see in other religions, and also see in Jesus. After all, Jesus himself made people of other faiths the heroes of his most famous stories (a Good Samaritan, for instance, and we will hear more about him, later; but also a Roman centurion and a Syrophoenician woman).

Jesus is the lens through which we see God. God had tried other ways of being made known. They didn't work.

Because we have been made free, we are free to reject as well as free to accept. That most famous of stories right at the beginning of the Bible, the story of Adam and Eve, is best understood as a story to explain why it is that we choose the wrong thing: the things that will harm us. In fact, most of what we call the Old Testament – the Hebrew Scriptures that are the first part of the Bible – is the story of how God chose a people through whom God's light and truth could be shown to everyone and by which we would learn to live for and with each other in the way that God intends, rather than let the perversity of self-interest drive us apart from each other and isolate us from God. Obviously, Christians believe that astonishing and precariously beautiful story reaches its climax in Jesus. Jewish people see it differently. They are still awaiting a Messiah. But both Jew and Christian would agree that God was employing and recruiting the people of Israel for a purpose that encompassed the whole world and every person, and that was about bringing peace to the human heart and peace to the world.

But I can hear the Christians who are reading this book object. They may well think I've got the writing of this book all round the wrong way. If what I have just said about Jesus is true, why have I waited until now to say it? Why have I spent several chapters talking about God without much reference to Jesus? And they would have a point.

However, since I'm also writing this book for people who are *not* followers of Jesus, but who may wish to examine the claims of the Christian faith, and since the only real way we can talk about Jesus is by talking about the things we know about him from the Bible, there is a danger that by saying this too soon, I will turn these readers away.

Therefore, if you are a reader who is not yet a follower of

Jesus, and who does not know the Bible, and who still suspects that any reference to it is a kind of special pleading, then I hope that approaching Jesus in this way has meant that you are still prepared to read a bit more.

This is not only why I have spoken about God first, but tried to speak about God with very little reference to the Bible or to any other so-called authoritative, religious document.

My starting point has been that, if it is true that God is the source of everything, and that God cares about everything, and that God has a purpose for everything, then there will be evidence of that in the things that God has created, and especially in us. What we do know, whether we believe in God or not, is that we have a privileged place of awesome responsibility within the inter-connected and inter-dependent ecology of the universe, and particularly our planet, and that our consciousness has developed in such a way that we have moral choices to make about how we inhabit the earth that can either be to the detriment of the earth (which, I'm afraid, is what we see around us at the moment) or to its healing and well-being. This vision of what the world could be, and the high ideals of love and self-sacrifice that are its motivation, are the image of the invisible God in us. In other words, we are approaching the *possibility of God* by examining the common experiences of love and the vision for a well-ordered world that are the raw materials of the inner life of everyone.

And, if you have kept reading, we have arrived at a point where the best explanation for the love that is inside us and that drives and motivates us, and even leads us to do things that are beyond self-interest and therefore not dictated purely by an instinct to survive or flourish, is God. Moreover, the Christian explanation of God – that God is love and that the whole creation is made from the outpouring of love that is itself flowing from that reciprocity of creative love that is the Godhead itself – seems to be the best explanation available: our conclusions about love correspond to the conclusions of the Christian faith. And where are those conclusions to be found? Well, it is in the Bible. That strange collection of books, predominantly the Hebrew Scriptures, which tell the story of how God's love chooses a people through whom that love can be made known to everyone. For Christians that story reaches its climax and its centre in the story of Jesus.

Therefore, you might now be inclined to at least *consider* that the claims of this book might be worth examining, even if, for the moment, it is just these few words: 'Jesus is the image of the invisible God . . . in him the fullness of God was pleased to dwell.'

But with these words in mind, when we now turn to the actual story of Jesus, we realise that everything we say about Jesus we are also saying about God.

It is God that is born in the stable at Bethlehem.

It is God who is teaching and healing and acting, confronting the political and religious conformities and presuppositions of his day.

It is God who dies on the cross.

It is God who is raised to life.

God is in Jesus, and therefore our humanity is joined to God and God is joined to us. Our flesh-and-blood humanity, and everything that it means to be human, is known by God. Jesus has become a meeting point, a place of union between humanity and God, between what we call heaven and what we know to be earth. And in the story of his dying and rising, even life and death are brought together.

If Jesus is just a good man, even the very best man that

ever lived, then his dying and even the story of his rising can have little benefit to us save as an example of goodness and an account of one person's vindication. But not ours. And if Jesus is *only* God, or God disguised as a human being, but not actually the one who shares the life of our humanity, then its meaning doesn't touch us. In fact, it is irrelevant. But if Jesus is, somehow, both *fully* God come down to earth, and *fully* human, our flesh fully inhabited by God, then it is God who has shared the fullness of life and the finality of dying. Moreover, in the story of his rising, we are risen too.

But you may not believe this story. You may still need some further explanation (though, as we know, proof itself cannot be on offer). And since it is the dying and rising of Jesus that is the heart and heartbeat of the story – the most bewilderingly strange and in human terms most difficult to believe – it is here we will turn next. However, we won't do it by simply re-telling the story in the Bible (though I dare to hope that before too long you may want to read this story for yourself), but by sticking to my method of telling the story without too much direct reference to the Scriptures. Let's turn instead to Smyrna in the year AD 155 and to the amazing tale of the martyrdom of Polycarp, its bishop.

CHAPTER NINE

Known as the pearl of the Aegean, the ancient city of Smyrna was the home to one of the seven churches mentioned in the Book of Revelation. There seems to have been a Christian community there from a very early date. It could well have been founded by Paul during what is known as his third missionary journey, in which we hear that Paul spent two years in this region following his arrival in Ephesus.[1] Ephesus is just along the coast from Smyrna. But we don't know for sure.

Smyrna is now the port city of Izmir on the Aegean Sea. With a population of nearly three million people, the city has the third largest population in Turkey. Consequently, there has not been much excavation of the ancient sites of this once-thriving Roman commercial centre, and before this a Greek city. However, the Roman remains that have been uncovered are magnificent.

Polycarp was the Bishop of Smyrna in AD 155. Like all Christian communities in this period, his church lived under the threat of persecution. On some occasions, such as the persecution under Nero following the Great Fire of Rome in AD 64, or the persecution under Diocletian in AD 303, this was systematic and brutal, but for long periods of time it was sporadic and local. However, it is well known and well documented that the Church was persecuted, as it still is today in some parts of the world. Many Christians lost their lives, sometimes in extreme and unspeakable ways. Christians – and many others – were thrown to lions.

All this only came to an end when, in AD 313, Constantine legalised the Christian religion, paving its way to becoming the official and only religion of the Roman Empire. But until then, the Christian faith couldn't help clashing with Rome. The ideas and beliefs at its heart threatened Roman hegemony. Christians swore allegiance to a different king and a different kingdom. They would not participate in the festivals that marked the feast days of the different gods that made up the state religion of Rome, still less pay homage to the emperor himself, who was viewed as a god. Christians had come to believe that Jesus Christ was Lord of all, not Caesar. This made them at best unpopular, but at worst, dangerous.

However, there was another, less obvious reason that Christians were mistrusted. They led a very distinctive life. They behaved differently. They followed a different ethical standard, and this was dangerous to the social cohesion of a society that was firmly entrenched and defined by caste, class and gender.

Christians were not trying to overthrow the rule of Rome, but by living so differently within the Roman jurisdiction and by politely but resolutely refusing to conform to some of its edicts and customs, Christianity offered a different way. It was also proving to be popular (hence the rapid spread of Christianity), particularly among the poor and the excluded.

A fascinating and articulate defence of Christianity survives from this period of spasmodic persecution. It is a letter from someone who calls himself Mathetes – though this is not the name of a person, but the Greek word for disciple – to someone called Diognetus. It may indeed have been written at exactly the same time that Polycarp was martyred. It too, like the account of the martyrdom, is one of the earliest surviving pieces of Christian literature outside of the Bible.

Forgive me for quoting from it at length, but by trying to demonstrate that Christians are not a threat to society, the letter also begins to explain why they had been *seen* as a threat and why – the subject that this book will eventually arrive at – the Christian faith has a radical vision for inhabiting the world differently. The unknown writer says this:

For Christians are distinguished from other men neither by country, nor language, nor the customs which they observe. For they neither inhabit cities of their own, nor employ a peculiar form of speech, nor lead a life which is marked out by any singularity. The course of conduct which they follow has not been devised by any speculation or deliberation of inquisitive men; nor do they, like some, proclaim themselves the advocates of any merely human doctrines. But, inhabiting Greek as well as barbarian cities, according as the lot of each of them has determined, and following the customs of the natives in respect to clothing, food, and the rest of their ordinary conduct, they display to us their wonderful and confessedly striking method of life. They dwell in their own countries, but simply as sojourners. As citizens, they share in all things with others, and yet endure all things as if foreigners. Every foreign land is to them as their native country, and every land of their birth as a land of strangers. They marry, as do all [others]; they beget children; but they do not destroy their offspring. They have a common table, but not a common bed. They are in the flesh, but they do not live after the flesh. They pass their days on earth, but they are citizens of heaven. They obey the prescribed laws, and at the same time surpass the laws by their lives. They love all men, and are persecuted by all. They are unknown and condemned; they are put to death, and restored to life. They are poor, yet make many rich; they are in lack of all things, and yet abound in all; they are dishonoured, and yet in their very dishonour are glorified. They are evil spoken of, and yet are justified; they are reviled, and bless; they are insulted, and repay the insult with honour; they do good, yet are punished as evil-doers. When punished, they rejoice as if quickened into life; they are assailed by the Jews as foreigners, and are persecuted by the Greeks; yet those who hate them are unable to assign any reason for their hatred.

To sum up all in one word – what the soul is in the body, that are Christians in the world.[2]

This remarkable passage describes the Christian life not just as a good and moral life, but as the life of what you might call a 'resident alien', living fully in and for the world, but knowing that true belonging lies elsewhere. It describes a life that is marked by a belonging to each other that transcends the usual barriers and definitions. Its currency is mercy and forgiveness. It speaks about this life as a journey home, but also of a mission to be the conscience and the compass of the world as the soul is for the body.

It is not surprising that such a life sounded like very good news to the poor and downtrodden, but very threatening to the privileged and powerful. Indeed, to them, it sounded revolutionary. The very fact that this letter was ever written shows just how misunderstood and reviled the Christian community had become in some quarters.

Which, in turn, led people back to the dangerous unbalancing of the status quo that Christianity appeared to advocate. Moreover, many people also believed that the pagan gods would not only be angered if they weren't worshipped properly: they would retaliate, bringing misfortune and judgement upon the people. Consequently, Christians were often blamed when bad things happened. Lynch mobs were formed.

Polycarp seems to have been gathered up in one of these more local persecutions. The eyewitness account of what happened, again written in the form of a letter, this time to the church at Philomelium, says that the local police commissioner, having arrested Polycarp, challenges him saying, 'Come now . . . where is the harm in just saying "Caesar is Lord", and offering the incense, and so forth, when it will save your life.'[3]

Such an apparently innocuous question also gets to the heart of the dis-ease Rome had with Christianity. Where does your true allegiance lie? With Christ or with Caesar?

Needless to say, Polycarp declines the offer. His life is based on the declaration that Jesus is Lord, and on everything else that follows from that. He was therefore brought before the Governor, no less a man than Lucius Statius Quadratus, the Proconsul of Asia (the richest of the Roman provinces), a post that I suppose might be similar in status and scope to that of a Victorian Viceroy to India. He, too, urges Polycarp to renounce his faith and save his life. 'Take the oath' – that is the oath to the Emperor – 'and I will let you go.' Finally, in exasperation he says to the bishop, 'Revile your Christ.'

Polycarp replies: 'Eighty and six years have I served him, and he has done me no wrong. How can I then blaspheme my King and my Saviour?'[4]

With this, Polycarp was condemned to death and burnt at the stake.

But how does this story help us to understand the death and resurrection of Jesus, which is my reason for telling you about Polycarp? Well, as they say in America, let's do the math.

Polycarp was almost certainly martyred in the year AD 155. We can be reasonably confident of this date, since the eyewitness, Marcion, tells us that the proconsul was Statius Quadratus and that it happened at 2:00 p.m. on the afternoon of the Greater Sabbath, and we can cross-reference these dates. He also tells us that it was 'seven days before the kalends of March',[5] which is 23 February (the day the Church still keeps as Polycarp's feast). However, and infuriatingly for modern readers, in the place in the narrative where you would expect the name and reign of the emperor to be noted, Marcion says 'the ruling monarch was Jesus Christ!' Consequently, we cannot be absolutely sure of the year: it could be the following year. Or it could be AD 168. But this doesn't much matter for my purposes. What I'm interested in is how Polycarp came to be a Christian.

Assuming the date of 155 for his martydom – the date most scholars agree on – and remembering he was eighty-six years old, and that he said he had served and followed Christ all his life, this means that Polycarp was born and baptised into a Christian family on the Adriatic coast of Asia Minor in the year AD 69, an astonishing thirty years or so after the death of Christ, in fact at about the same time that Paul was in prison in Rome writing his letters. But even a date thirteen years later is still astonishingly early.

Somehow the story of Jesus Christ, and in particular the story of his dying and rising, has spread across the world so that even in a place like Smyrna, miles away from Jerusalem and shaped by very different religious ideas and beliefs, a child is born into a Christian family, is baptised and brought up in the Christian faith, even under persecution, and goes on to become their bishop. How could such ideas spread? Especially in the teeth of persecution, first by some of the Jewish religious leaders in the birthplace of Christianity, Palestine itself, and then by the officials of Rome and by local people who saw it as a threat to the status quo?

And who was doing the spreading? Well, it was a motley band of illiterate peasant fishermen, political zealots, misfits, the odd tax collector, one or two senior Jewish religious officials, and most surprising of all for a culture that was very definitely led by men, a few very significant women. (In fact, when you turn to the Scriptures, you will find that women were the only ones who stood at the cross and were the first witnesses to the resurrection.)

If this was a master plan for global domination or a blue-print for communicating ideas across the world, it wouldn't look good on paper or win many endorsements. The very people who, in the main, had proved their unsuitability for the task through their painful ignorance and shocking cowardice, all falling away at the very time Jesus needed them most, are now entrusted with the task of taking this message to the ends of the earth.

But they succeed. Churches are established all over the place. Not yet buildings, or even the other infrastructures of church life with which most of us are familiar, but meeting in homes and in small groups, and where necessary in secret, debating their cause in whatever forums presented themselves, and demonstrating a radical love of God and of neighbour. Regardless of status or religion, the Church grew. It soon burst out of its Jewish womb, and Greeks and others, often slaves and the poor, became part of the first Christian communities. (Another of those letters that Paul writes from prison was about granting freedom to a slave.)

So what was this message? Well, it was indeed about loving God and loving neighbour. And it did suggest a new world order in which we are born again into a new humanity and where the old definitions no longer count, but at heart it was a staggeringly simple proclamation about God, and it was from this that everything else followed.

The first Christians said – and, sorry, I'm quoting from the Bible again, but this is the simplest and best way of telling you what this first proclamation was all about:

> Jesus of Nazareth, a man attested to you by God with deeds of power . . . whom you crucified . . . God raised him up, having freed him from death, because it was impossible for him to be held in its power . . . Therefore let the entire House of Israel know with certainty that God has made him both Lord and Messiah, this Jesus whom you crucified.[6]

This is Peter speaking in the streets to Jewish people who would have been in Jerusalem when Jesus was crucified. He also emphasises that he is a witness to this, i.e. that he has seen Jesus risen from the dead.

This assertion that God has raised Jesus from the dead, which Peter and the other disciples are saying makes him the Messiah (that is, the Lord and Saviour that all Israel has been waiting for), is the starting point and the foundation of the Christian faith. It is because Jesus has been raised from the dead that those who follow him now affirm that Jesus is the image of the invisible God, the one who comes to us from God. It is because Jesus is risen from the dead that they are reformed as a new humanity, what they describe at the time, initially, as a new Israel. It is this that leads them to a new ethic and a new vision. This does not deny or compete with the old vison that God had made known to Israel. It completes it and fulfils it. And it is because Jesus is risen from the dead that they do not fear the judgement or the persecution or the ridicule of the world. The one who died on the cross is alive, and that 'aliveness' has re-charged them and motivated them and led them to take hold of everything else they know about Jesus.

This new experience of God is not just about the resurrection, but, because of the resurrection, God is now available in new ways. They call this the Holy Spirit. The abiding and motivating presence of the risen Jesus remains with them, but is now unconfined by time and place. God had been with them in his earthly life and ministry (though they mostly didn't realise it), but inevitably that presence had been limited. Jesus was, as I have been at pains to point out, a real human being, and therefore subject to the limitations of time and space that all human beings experience. But in his risen life, Jesus is unconstrained. He can be equally and completely with the disciples in Jerusalem and remain with them, completely and unreservedly, as they take his message across the world. This is the work and activity of the Holy Spirit, the spirit of love. As we observed earlier, love does not need to be rationed. It is always completely available. It replenishes itself by being shared. Consequently, it was this experience of Jesus risen from the dead and the presence of Jesus with them through the Spirit that not only enabled that unpromising band of disciples to do the amazing things they did: it compelled them.

There are, I suppose, other explanations of how the Christian faith could have spread to Smyrna in such a short space of time. But since we know for sure, without having to turn to the Bible, that the first Christians did indeed risk their lives to travel the known world telling people that Jesus had risen from the dead and that in him a new relationship with God was possible and that God's very nature was love and that this changed everything about how we ordered the world, it is actually quite hard to imagine what they can be.

Would you risk your life to share a message you knew was false? Or if, somehow, all the disciples, and many others, were hoodwinked into believing this story, or suffered from some mass delusion, or were even seized by a very strong inner conviction that Jesus, though dead, was still with them, *as if he were alive*, then I still don't see how that explains the rapidity and consistency and steady accumulating growth of the Church in those days. So much so that Polycarp is born into a family who are already Christians; he is baptised and, despite persistent persecution, continues in the way of Christ.

This isn't proof. Those other explanations could be true. Those first disciples could have been deluded or delusional. They could have just made it up. There could have been some mass hallucination. It could have been invented years later and the whole story back-filled. They could have just believed Jesus was with them, and this drove them on. But, for me, none of these explanations quite match the facts – the facts, that is, that we can observe without opening the Bible: the simple facts of Christianity's growth.

Therefore, I have come to an astonishing conclusion. I have concluded that the most amazing explanation is, in fact, the right one: that which is most incredible is also most credible. And it is this: Jesus, who is the image of the invisible God, and in whom the fullness of God was dwelling, was born a human being just like you and me, died on the cross and was raised to life by God as a sign of our destiny as those who are beloved of God, and of the new relationship we have with God whom we discover is love, and of the new humanity and the new way of inhabiting the earth that the Christian faith proclaims.

But without the resurrection, this story is nothing. We could still live by the fine ideals of the Christian faith, and that would be good, but there would be no personal hope for us beyond this life.

Furthermore, without this hope and the way it anchors us to a set of values and ideals that can guide and shape our lives, there is the ever-present danger that we human beings will start living only for ourselves or build barriers around ourselves or blame and scapegoat others. Long term, sacrificial policies for safeguarding the environment, or building systems of care, or investing in justice, will be the first to slip from the agenda. And if what is worst in us, a self-regarding false north of hubris and conceit, is allowed to overwhelm other narratives and ideals, then gas chambers and pogroms are not far behind. Or bullying, exploitation of the vulnerable, and violence. Sadly, all of human history, be it the dictatorships of religion or politics, or the everyday cruelties of abuse, show this clearly. There is a deadening potential for darkness in the human spirit, a rage and fury that could boil over and consume the world, starting with the helpless and the poor. The seeds of this horror are always waiting in the ground of our being. They are watered by neglect, envy, pride, vanity and greed. In every human community and in every human heart you can see them starting to blossom.

But because Jesus is risen from the dead, there is hope – hope for us, hope for our world. We can turn to the things Jesus said and the things Jesus did with a new confidence, for through Jesus, God the creator *of* the world is speaking *to* the world, showing us how we should live, uprooting what is false and hateful within us and teaching us a different way. This is the way of Jesus Christ that I was trying to point that young woman on Paddington Station towards. Only there wasn't time to say all this!

We can, therefore, at this point, if we wish, open our Bibles and although we will not dwell for too long on the teaching, the life and the death of Jesus – you can find out more about this elsewhere – we will look at the story of Jesus as a way of making the final turn of our journey: how might this hope change the world? How might we live differently?

CHAPTER TEN

In this chapter we will start to look briefly at what Jesus said and did. There are one or two small references to this outside of the Bible, but of course the Bible has to be the primary source. I just hope that having read so far you are at least prepared to carry on suspending your disbelief and, for the time being, take these texts at face value.

But to bolster your confidence there are, by the way, all sorts of very good reasons why we *can* consider the biblical texts as reliable source documents. First of all, there are more than four thousand different ancient Greek manuscripts (Greek is the language in which the New Testament was written) containing either all the New Testament or portions of it. Written on papyrus or parchment, these manuscripts survived. We still uncover ancient documents written on these materials today. They last.

Some of them are very old, dating back to between AD 180 and AD 225. The oldest we have comes from AD 130. This is still some time after the death and resurrection of Christ, but common sense, as well as solid academic scholarship, tells us that the story of Jesus was not written down immediately. Stories were passed on orally, as we know was the case in many cultures at that time. Moreover, most of Jesus' first followers would not have been able to read or write anyway. We also know that ancient documents like these were written by hand and then copied. Therefore, although we know that

Paul was writing his letters in about AD 60, the earliest surviving remnants and complete copies we have date to about a hundred years later. But the fact that they were copied says something else. They were considered to be precious and important. Furthermore, from about the same very early period of the Church's life, when it was still under persecution, we find literally thousands of quotations from the New Testament in the writings of the people known as the early Church Fathers (people like Polycarp): those who followed the apostles as the first leaders and teachers of the Church. The earliest of these surviving letters is from Clement of Rome, who was writing in AD 96. Indeed, it has been observed that if every copy of the New Testament disappeared from the earth, it would be possible to reconstruct the entire New Testament with quotes from the Church Fathers, with only fifteen or twenty verses not mentioned.

Finally, the New Testament as we know it did not reach its final form until the Councils of Hippo and Carthage in the years AD 393 and 397.

Again, none of this is proof that what the New Testament says is true, only evidence that what Christians say about Jesus is consistent and goes right back to the first people who knew him and followed him. The books of the New Testament are a reliable witness to this. But because we live in a cynical age, this reliability is often called into question.

The archaeological and scholarly facts tell a different story. They show that actually many New Testament documents can be dated back to a comparatively short time after the events they describe. In fact, there is more evidence for the very early existence of the New Testament than there is for other ancient documents whose reliability is rarely questioned. So, for instance, *The Histories of Herodotus*, a work of huge scholarly significance for the origins of the Greco-Persian wars and for the whole concept of writing investigative historical narrative, was written between fifty to a hundred years after the events it describes and the earliest surviving copy is from AD 900, that is *1,400 years later*. But very few people doubt the reliability of the text. Similarly, Plutarch's famous *Lives of the Roman Emperors*, another widely referenced historical work, includes stories of people who lived 600 years before Plutarch was writing. The earliest surviving manuscript is from AD 950.

I could give you many other examples. Most ancient documents, whose reliability we do not question, describe events that happened hundreds of years before the surviving manuscripts we have to study. We trust them because we know and assume that there were earlier copies. We understand and accept the processes that lay behind the copies we have. But when it comes to the New Testament, even though we have hundreds of copies, and even though some of them are written less than two hundred years after the events they describe, their reliability is often questioned or dismissed. This is a mistake that only a little historical investigation soon corrects.

So what does the New Testament tell us about Jesus: who he is, and what he said and did?

I have already quoted Paul's description of Jesus as the image of the invisible God. St John, the writer of the Fourth Gospel, uses an equally striking image. He says that in Jesus the 'word was made flesh'. The 'word' he is referring to is the Greek word *logos*, which is rather more than 'a word' in the way we use it in English, but 'an idea', 'a philosophy', and 'an identity'. John is saying that the word of God, that is the will, the wisdom and the purpose and power of God through which the whole universe came into being, has, in

Jesus, become flesh. Our flesh. Therefore, as we have explored, Christians understand Jesus to be both a complete human being *and* completely God dwelling in and through a human being.

Jesus is born into a human family and into a faith and a culture. As we are. For Jesus it is the Jewish faith and the Jewish culture, those people who had always understood themselves to be chosen by God in order to bring God's light, justice and peace to the world.

For thirty years we know hardly anything about Jesus' life. His identity and his person were hidden, though it is reasonable to speculate that he was meditating upon his vocation and calling. This doesn't mean he knew in advance exactly what was going to happen to him. If he did, then he would be something other than completely human. It was probably more an inner conviction growing in him (and we all experience inner convictions of one sort or another from time to time) that his life was to be the vehicle through which God was finally going to restore the lost relationship with the world.

Because he wanted to demonstrate solidarity with the human race, he is baptised by his cousin, John, in the River Jordan. Baptism was a sign of repentance, that is, an acknowledgement of past failures and a willingness to live differently. John was calling people to re-orientate their lives and return to God. Jesus is the one person who doesn't need to do this, but he *chooses* to do so to show that he doesn't just represent God to humanity, he represents humanity to God. So his public ministry begins.

His teaching is rooted in the Jewish tradition that he knows by heart. But he gives it a new edge. People say of him that he speaks with authority. I'm not sure that's quite what they meant. He spoke with authenticity. The words he said matched the life he led. This is a powerful combination. It breeds real authority: the authority of a transparent life where words and actions are one harmonious expression of inner intent and there is nothing to hide. It is beautiful and compelling. Unsurprisingly, people followed him. They still do.

But as well as words, there were powerful deeds. Surprising and inexplicable things happened. Water was turned into wine. Hungry people were fed. Sick people were healed. To the modern reader all this is somewhat troubling. We might like to believe it is true, but it goes against the grain of the world we know. All I can repeat is that this is the consistent witness of the New Testament writers. God is in Jesus, and therefore he does things that are inexplicable to the world *as it is*, but point towards the new normal of the world as *God wants it to be*. It is as if a future world is breaking into the present.

Perhaps even the writers of the New Testament struggled with understanding these inexplicable things. It would be funny if they didn't. After all, it would be a very contemporary arrogance to assume that simple-minded people at the time believed things that we sophisticated people could not believe now. People were dumbfounded by Jesus. They saw in him things that they had not seen in anyone else. In him, God seemed to be transparently at work. They hadn't quite reached the point where they felt able to call him 'god'. But they edged towards this. So, in John's Gospel the word 'miracle' isn't used. John calls these things 'signs'. They point to something beyond themselves. If it helps, think of them as signposts to a new reality and a new ordering of the world where the hungry are fed and the sick are healed and war, injustice and famine are no more.

But even if some people started to wonder about Jesus' identity, most people didn't know who he was. Often they latched on to the signs, but disregarded or misunderstood the person who was giving them. This might explain why sometimes, having healed a person, Jesus asked them not to tell anyone about it. This was hardly practical. How was a blind man supposed to keep quiet about the fact that he could now see! But it does suggest that even Jesus himself is anxious that we do not linger for too long with the miraculous. It is the new reality and new ordering of the world that this points towards that is what matters to him. It is what he calls in his teaching, the kingdom of God.

There is one momentous moment in the story when Jesus actually asks his disciples who they think he is. Most of them assume he is a prophet, like the great prophets they knew about. But Peter suddenly gets it, even though its implications are still unclear to him. He says Jesus is the Christ – that is, the anointed one, the Messiah – the one that Israel has been waiting for and through whom God will act decisively. Interestingly, before this point in the story, only the demons that Jesus casts out seem to know who he is. Or, just as interesting, the little people on the edge of the story. People who were not considered either worthy or important, such as women, children and foreigners, were often the ones who seemed to get Jesus and to whom he reached out.

However, if the mention of demons so hot on the trail of miracles is causing you alarm – even if you do accept the different thought world of the times in which these documents were written and the particular new reality that is present to us in Jesus – let us look at what Jesus said. For his words about the kingdom of God reach through the centuries and are like fresh, clear water from a spring, quenching our thirst for love, truth and hope. Though also challenging us to live differently.

There are far too many for me to go through them all. I'm really hoping you'll want to read them for yourself at some point. I'm also aware that some of these stories and sayings have passed into our culture. For example, some of us will be familiar with phrases like 'Good Samaritan' and 'Prodigal Son'. We might even know the stories.

So let me start with the first of those: the story of the Good Samaritan. It is a story through which we can see Jesus' whole radical agenda of love.

It begins with a question. And, at that, a question from a lawyer, a person who deals in both precision and nuance, someone who likes things defined and neatly tied down, but who also, being familiar with human frailty and wrongdoing, recognises that one size rarely fits all: general principles, however universal, need local application. As is the way with lawyers, he opens with a broad question to draw Jesus in: 'Teacher,' he asks, 'what must I do to inherit eternal life?'

Jesus replies – as he often does – with another question: 'What is written in the law? What do you read there?'

The lawyer, who obviously knows the law, responds correctly: 'You shall love the Lord your God with all your heart, and with all your soul, and with all your strength, and with all your mind; and your neighbour as yourself.'[1]

Let's pause for a moment. The lawyer's answer is profoundly beautiful. In fact, the lawyer is quoting back to Jesus words he uses himself on other occasions to summarise the whole of the Jewish law. I quoted them in an earlier chapter. It is about three things: loving God; loving yourself; and loving your neighbour. And to do these things with your whole being, that is your whole person with all its faculties of intellect, imagination and will: all your heart, all your soul, all your strength and all your mind.

It is a striking summary of the law. Indeed, when Jesus says these words in another place in the Gospels, he adds that to love God like this is the greatest of the commandments, the second being to love your neighbour as yourself. He says that 'on these two commandments hang all the law and the prophets'.[2] That is the whole Jewish tradition of which he is a part and which he comes to fulfil.

However, Jesus is not saying anything particularly new. He summarises it brilliantly, but it is what the Jewish faith and, indeed, other faith traditions have always taught. It may be misunderstood. It is often neglected. But it is the faith of which he is a part.

Perhaps the particular emphasis on love of self needs unpacking before we get to the nub of the story, which is the question about who exactly is my neighbour.

We do need to love ourselves. Insights from contemporary psychology show us how damaging it is when we don't. We are also aware of how poverty, abuse, neglect and lack of opportunity stunt our growth and lead to all sorts of mental dis-ease where we can even end up hating ourselves.

Jesus speaks of a totality of love, properly affirming that unless we love ourselves, we are unlikely ever to be able to love anyone else, let alone God. We need to recognise this, and commit ourselves to providing affirmation and opportunity to those who have been neglected, as well as acknowledging that we live in a very hedonistic age in which there is too much of the wrong sort of self-referential love, which leads us to imagine that we are at the centre of everything and to so obsess about ourselves that we become the abusers and neglecters.

So, before we turn to the lawyer's second question, and in order to help us understand what it means to love ourselves properly, let us think about the inter-relationship between loving self and loving God and being able to love others.

A thousand years after Jesus (it often takes the Church a long time to work things out!) Bernard of Clairvaux spoke about four degrees of love:

1. Love of self for self's sake.
2. Love of God for self's sake.
3. Love of God for God's sake.
4. Love of self for God's sake.

In other words, we move through different degrees of love, beginning with a simple and self-referential love of self with self at the centre.

Then we may become aware of God and also start to love God, but only so far as it serves self.

Then there is what I suppose we might call a 'religious' way of looking at things, in which we falsely and unhelpfully deny self and try to pretend it is only about God. The danger here is that what looks like piety can quickly become extremism. It is not just self that is denied: it is neighbour as well, and all the needs of the world are simply ignored. Fanaticism starts to foment. Please remember what the young woman at Paddington Station said to me: 'some people embrace their faith so tightly it frightens everyone else away'. It is from such well-intentioned religiosity that pogroms, inquisitions and the like sometimes begin. But it can be a brief stage in the growth of love, not only a dangerous resting place.

Finally, there is the highest degree of love – what Jesus

speaks about and what the lawyer also comprehends. This is where we love self, but not for self's sake. We do it in recognition and honour of the God without whom there would be no self. It is the love and the meaning and outpouring of love that this whole book is written to describe and commend as the means by which hearts are changed. 'Such love', wrote Bernard, 'is the fountain of life, and the soul which does not drink from it cannot be alive.'[3]

The lawyer in this story seems to get this. So Jesus says to him, 'You have given the right answer; do this, and you will live.'

So now the lawyer tightens the focus of his question. 'Who is my neighbour?' he asks.

And Jesus replies with a story. This is significant. When he is expounding general principles, he is clear and succinct in his teaching. But when it comes to their application, he usually either tells a story or, in some instances, does something himself to illustrate what the meaning might be (like washing his disciples' feet). And the good thing about stories is that in order to understand them you need to get inside them. The truth of the story cannot be neatly extracted. You have to have the story itself. You have to get inside it and be part of it. You have to feel it as well as theorise about it. Moreover, the story can hold more than one truth in tension. It can have different interpretations. In fact, by telling the story and by inviting us to enter into the story, Jesus invites us to become our own moral philosopher, working out what the story might mean for us and for our world.

This is the clever and engaging way that Jesus teaches us. It is not just because it is a good way of teaching (as all good teachers will know), it is because, with Jesus, the message can never be separated from the messenger, for the one who is speaking to us is God come down to earth. God wants us to live differently, but at the heart of this different way of living is a new set of relationships, and those relationships are with God as well as with self and others. We will most learn how to love when we allow God to love us. Therefore, the deliberate ambiguity of Jesus' method is both to get us to work at the answer, and to draw us closer in relationship. You can't just take the story away. You follow the storyteller for more.

So, who is my neighbour? Well, the answer gets us right to the heart of the Christian way of inhabiting the world and it is not very comfortable.

So, for starters, please note that Jesus doesn't tell us to 'love everyone'. He suggests something much harder: love your neighbour; love that very irritating and particular someone who is next to you right now. Especially the ones who seem most unlovable. Even the ones that you have invested most in not loving at all. And he illustrates it with a story that brings the abstract and universal notion of 'loving everyone' to specific, emotional, prickly and powerful life.

A man was travelling from Jerusalem to Jericho and fell among thieves. He is mugged, beaten and left for dead in a ditch. The story then proceeds like so many good stories do, with a familiar and predictable set-up and since there isn't a culture anywhere that doesn't enjoy poking fun at the establishment it, unsurprisingly, does this by enjoying the failures of a cast of important and, more tellingly, self-important and self-serving people who should know better: the very people who often pronounce on the moral life, and sit in judgement on others, but who don't practise what they preach and whose feet of clay are now triumphantly revealed. One by one, they pass by on the other side, leaving the man in the ditch alone, terrified and without aid: first a priest, then a lawyer, which must have stung the particular lawyer listening, especially as he had done so well with his first answers. When the time for action comes, when they need to put their money where their mouth is, these pillars and representatives of the universal laws fail to do what the law, and what even common decency, requires. They don't stop to help the man. They save their own skin instead. They don't get involved.

And at this point, just as if I'd told a story beginning, 'There was an Englishman, a Scotsman and an Irishman . . .', even if you didn't know the joke, you'd know where the joke is heading. The Irishman is being set up for a fall. The casual racism upon which these jokes rely is still common in our society and prevalent in every society. In Ireland, I gather, they tell jokes about people from Kerry. So we, too, listening to the story, and especially those first listeners, know where the story is going. The hero is going to be the common man, a good, ordinary Jew succeeding where the priest and the lawyer fail.

Only it's not like that. For the next person to come along is a Samaritan. And here the power of the story is lost unless you also know, as those first listeners would certainly have done, that a Samaritan is a hated foreigner. Not just any old foreigner, but a heretic. For the Samaritans, who live next door to the Jews, make rival claims, saying they are the true inheritors of the promises to Abraham. They have even set up a rival temple on Mount Gerizim. They are the enemy. Jews don't just avoid Samaritans. It is unclean to mix with them, such were the ritual prohibitions by which they lived, prohibitions and customs that also illustrate the way societies are usually ordered with all sorts of protocols and customs to keep some people in and make sure others are out. Some of these are overt. Some are not. Often the most invidious are hidden, but just as conclusive. This is why black lives matter, not simply all lives matter. All lives matter is true and obvious, but with little challenge. Black lives matter rubs against the unconscious and disturbs the assumed normalcy of whiteness.

So this is Jesus' hero: the person you look down on; the person who is not like you; the person you avoid; the person who is unclean; the person whom you have been brought up to despise. And in a moment, Jesus, the master storyteller, twists the storytelling blade in up to the hilt, for we find out that this most unwelcome, odious and unlikely companion is not just an enemy, but a *rich* enemy as well. He lifts the injured man out of the ditch. He binds up his wounds. He puts him on his donkey. He takes him to an inn. He covers all the costs and promises to return in case there is more to pay.

This really is an extremely uncomfortable little story, for with Jesus having made fun of those in power and of their foibles, and with his listeners being unable to associate with the hero of the story, there is no one left to identify with except the man in the ditch, the wounded and beaten victim whose sworn enemy turns out to be neighbour and friend.

If you want to understand the power of the story for our world today, it is the local BNP councillor being helped by the wealthy Pakistani businessman; it is the prime minister of Israel in the ditch and a rebel Hamas fighter giving him mouth-to-mouth resuscitation. It is Donald Trump finding himself on the wrong side of his own wall, with all his papers stolen, and an illegal Mexican immigrant helping him out. But don't think it doesn't apply to you as well. Think of the person from whom you would least want to receive mercy and kindness, where you would rather stay in the ditch and die than be helped by that person, and you have the power of the narrative: a story, not a moral proposition, to tell you what loving neighbour looks like.

As it turns out, Jesus hasn't actually answered the question at all. The lawyer asks, 'Who is my neighbour?' and Jesus replies by showing who is neighbour to him. The lawyer wants to know whom he should be good to. Jesus shows him whom he will receive from. Jesus emphasises who is your neighbour *now*; it is in this moment – the time of trial when we are in need or when we see someone else in need – that our vocation to self-forgetful love is enacted and revealed.

It is a powerful story. It speaks across the centuries. It is as relevant today as it was yesterday. It will carry on being relevant tomorrow. Jesus shines a light on the limitations of our love, on our tribalism and racism, our imagined superiority, our unwillingness to get involved, and the many different ways that we walk by on the other side and so collude with injustice. And in all that follows we find out that Jesus himself is the one who has come to rescue us. He is our Good Samaritan, who is looking out for us when everything else lets us down.

CHAPTER ELEVEN

By telling the story of the Good Samaritan – and in many other stories that reveal different aspects of this new way of living – Jesus demonstrates that to follow him and to live his way requires us to enter freely into a set of relationships with others where everyone is our neighbour. So he says elsewhere – and here he really is contrasting the keeping of the law that defined the faithfulness of the Old Testament with a new commandment to love that exceeds and fulfils this:

> 'You have heard that it was said, "An eye for an eye and a tooth for a tooth." But I say to you, Do not resist an evildoer. But if anyone strikes you on the right cheek, turn the other also; and if anyone wants to sue you and take your coat, give your cloak as well; and if anyone forces you to go one mile, go also the second mile.
>
> 'You have heard that it was said, "You shall love your neighbour and hate your enemy." But I say to you, Love your enemies and pray for those who persecute you, so that you may be children of your Father in heaven.'[1]

This profoundly challenging teaching includes the phrase 'so that you may be children of your Father in heaven'. In other words, you are going to be most like God when you love each other. In fact, if you read on, it gets more challenging still. Jesus says: 'Be perfect, therefore, as your heavenly Father is perfect.'[2]

Of course, perfection is beyond us. And perfectionism, which often means giving up if we can't be perfect, and tormenting ourselves in the process, is a curse. But perhaps Jesus means that by opening ourselves up to that new set of relationships that he makes available, we can grow into that maturity of love where we end up truly loving ourselves and our neighbour, but for God's sake, for the sake of God's holistic and wholesome vision for the world.

These words are found in the longest teaching passage in the Gospels, what is known as the Sermon on the Mount. You can find it in Matthew's Gospel, chapters 5–7.

It begins with a mysteriously beautiful passage known as the Beatitudes.

Here Jesus sets out a series of maxims that at first sight seem to be his equivalent of the Ten Commandments. Like Moses, the Old Testament prophet who received the latter, when Jesus receives the Beatitudes he has gone up a mountain. And like Moses he has a series of short, pithy things to say that will then need a lifetime to work out.

However, the Beatitudes are not a moral code. They are not things you can either do or not do. They are attitudes to which we can aspire. Rather than describing the moral life, a code by which we can justly live alongside each other in society, they describe, using Jesus' words quoted above, what it looks like to 'go the second mile'. They describe what perfect love in action looks like.

Here they are:

Blessed are the poor in spirit, for theirs is the kingdom of heaven.
Blessed are those who mourn, for they will be comforted.
Blessed are the meek, for they will inherit the earth.

Blessed are those who hunger and thirst for righteousness,
for they will be filled.

Blessed are the merciful, for they will receive mercy.

Blessed are the pure in heart, for they will see God.

Blessed are the peacemakers, for they will be called children of God.

Blessed are those who are persecuted for righteousness'
sake, for theirs is the kingdom of heaven.[3]

I don't propose to spend ages unpacking these; it would require another book. But alongside the Ten Commandments themselves, the Lord's Prayer and the Creed, the Beatitudes have become one of the central documents of the Church. As I have already said, living by them is the work of a lifetime.

They are the centre of Jesus' teaching. Their meaning, however, isn't always self-evident. Like his stories, they need inhabiting.

They are very challenging. It isn't easy to be merciful. It isn't easy to make peace. Especially if the likely outcome is the persecution we usually make efforts to avoid. Not that there is anything good about persecution. As we know, mockery and ridicule hurt. How much more hurtful is it to be hunted down because of your witness to peace? Nevertheless, it is witnesses to peace that Jesus is recruiting here. His own life, and everything that he teaches, led this way: to the peace that is beyond the world's understanding and is about a wholeness and totality of giving and receiving love.

Jesus is inviting us to live with a different set of attitudes. And he does not baulk from acknowledging that these attitudes will bring us into conflict with the carefully protected interests of those who secure power and influence for themselves at the expense of peace. They exchange it for what is little more than a truce. At best, an absence of war, where we live in our jealously guarded siloes and forcibly protect our borders, repelling intruders and stamping on those who even dream differently.

In our own society, thankfully, we enjoy freedoms of speech and action. This means that we rarely meet with much opposition beyond people's unreflective apathy or polished disdain. But these freedoms we enjoy should not be taken for granted. They have been hard won. They could easily be lost. Especially if we fail to see where they have come from: precisely this realisation of the dignity and worth of every person and our responsibilities to each other that arose through Christ.

Unfortunately, these things that underpin what is best in our society are not self-evidently the best. We've got so used to them that we easily imagine they are. But actually, we don't observe them in the world around us. Nature, for instance, is not democratic. Nor particularly caring. The weakest usually die first. The fittest survive. Nor is it much different in human communities. Our history – always written by those who win – is one bloody story of conquest after another. Empires rise and fall, and there is very little to suggest that there might be another kingdom where a different set of values prevails, and where the king turns out to be the servant of all. But that is precisely the Christian narrative. It is a golden thread running through human history. In every age it can either be held on to, or cut away; left to our own devices, especially when our backs are to the wall, we find that the human compass is usually set towards self-preservation. Our empires and systems are usually designed to keep others out. Or at least in their place, so that they can serve us. In this so-called 'real world', shepherds do not go in search of one lost sheep, as Jesus suggested God does, in one of his parables. That would be uneconomic. Like the rest of us, they play a percentages game, and for the sake of the ninety-nine, we accept the loss of the one. The strongest and the wiliest prevail. That's just how it is, we say. If we can help the weak, we will. But if we can't, or if it affects us badly, we won't and we don't.

This is why the world needs a set of values – and a story – that will save us from ourselves, and our worst instincts. This is why we need a set of values that are rooted in a tradition whose stories and whose very heart are, gloriously, the life and teaching of a person who is himself the revelation of God's love and purposes for the world he made and loves – who even laid down his life to search out those who are lost: the very image of the invisible God. More than that: someone who loves us and knows what it is like to be us, who has experienced from the inside just what it is like to inhabit a divided and compromised world.

Therefore, the Beatitudes are a set of values and attitudes by which we can inhabit the world differently and through which we can begin to see what matters in the world and what must be done.

The Beatitudes describe what it means to live as a child of the God who is love and in God's commonwealth of love in action. They are anchored in Jesus' own life and ministry. So, if you have difficulty in understanding what any one of them means, the best way of finding an answer is to look to Jesus himself and see how he lives this beatitude out.

Perhaps because it is the first beatitude, and in many respects the doorway into all the others, but also the trickiest to understand, let's dwell for a moment with what it means to be poor in spirit. It means, I suppose, not to put yourself at the centre. It means not to take yourself too seriously. Not to be self-sufficient. Not to be overly self-reliant. Being poor in your own spirit opens up the possibility of being rich in God.

This is a profoundly counter-intuitive rebuttal of so many of the things we prize. In fact, the whole Christian narrative reckons that the basic human dilemma is that we imagine ourselves to be at the centre of things and that it is, by ousting God from God's proper place, that all the other horrors of the world proceed. For if I am at the centre, everyone else is easily relegated to a walk-on part in the central narrative of the universe, which is my life. And since God was, so we imagine, so easy to topple from his throne, God probably never existed anyway: this life is all there is, and therefore seeking my own pleasure and well-being is not such a moral abdication after all. As long as I don't hurt anyone, what does it matter if there are people starving elsewhere? Or living under oppression. What can I do about it? How can my small voice make a difference? It's a pity. But that's the way the world is. Nothing can change it.

But things can change! That is what we are discovering in this book. One person can make a difference. God isn't toppled. God was from the very beginning the one whose name is love and who in order for love to be fulfilled, and because it is the very nature of love to beget love, created a universe in which we are capable of putting self first if we wish. But in Jesus we are shown another way.

We can accept and embrace this way. Or we are free to reject it.

And of course, that's precisely what happened.

Even those who got it, didn't, at first, get it enough to face persecution. Or even enquiry. They ran away instead. They pretended they never even knew Jesus.

On the night before he died, Jesus had a meal with those first followers and, breaking bread and sharing wine, he said that these were his body and his blood. They couldn't understand what he meant. But what he was showing them was an acted parable of what his death the next day would mean. His body would be broken. His blood would be shed. Jesus would live out the Beatitudes. His poverty of spirit, which meant his reliance on God; his dogged determination to put God first and to be guided and shaped by God's purpose; his crying out for justice and mercy; his meekness and purity of vision; his aching desire for peace: all led him into confrontation with those whose vested interests his vision threatened.

He says to his disciples that he is giving them a new commandment: they must love one another. He says it is by this love that people will know that they are his followers. He even says that the greatest love of all is a love that goes the second mile by relinquishing self-interest and self-preservation and laying itself down for those it loves.

Such love is hard. But it is not necessarily so hard for us to imagine. We human beings, whom I believe are made in God's image and therefore, at our best, capable of self-forgetful and even self-sacrificial love, can imagine that we might lay down our lives for those we love: our children; our partner; our dearest friends. But in a magnificent passage from his letter to the Church in Rome, Paul acknowledges that even this love is rare: 'though perhaps for a good person someone might actually dare to die'. But, he continues, capturing in a single sentence what Christians believe about the death of Jesus: 'God proves his love for us in that while we still were sinners Christ died for us.'[4]

I don't think I've used the word sin yet in this book. It can be an off-putting word for people today. But don't dismiss it too quickly. At one level all it describes is the fact that we all fall short. This isn't particularly a religious idea: we all fall short of our own standards. This happens almost every day when we berate ourselves for saying this or doing that. The Christian faith adds to this very human estimation of our failures, the values and standards of God: the love we see in Jesus. We end up *not* being poor in spirit, *not* being merciful, *not* hungering and thirsting for what is right. This isn't merely breaking the rules of a moral code (though we may do this as well!). It is failing to be the very best we can be because we have allowed love of self and putting self first to squeeze out that better way of living that we know will bring peace to the world, but may also bring us persecutions and hardships along the way.

So we settle for something else. This is the grim reality of sin: not just the bad things we do, but a whole culture of division, in which we are set against each other, and therefore set against God.

Thus it has always been the case that following Jesus isn't easy. It can and does bring us into conflict with the vested interests of the world. It led Jesus to a cross. And he himself said to his followers that they will have to carry crosses as well, sharing in the very misunderstandings, jealousies and hatreds that led to his execution.

He plumbs the depths of our own alienation from God and takes upon himself the consequences of all our wrong choices. He shows us what sacrificial love looks like. He offers forgiveness. He forgives the soldiers who nailed him to the cross. He reaches out to the criminals who hang beside him. He forgives us. What looks to the world to be a wretched and meaningless defeat – one more death among so many – turns out to be victory. It is the victory of love and forgiveness over hatred and resentment.

As we know, if we have been wronged, no one can forgive the perpetrator on our behalf. Or if they do, that forgiveness has no currency. Only the victim has the power to forgive. So Jesus becomes the victim. His death, it turns out, is the ultimate dismantling of those barriers of separation that kept us from God and kept us from each other. Our wrongdoing and all the wrongdoings and failures of the world are confronted in the God who in Jesus becomes victim for us. Jesus, at his dying, even cries out in anguish that God had abandoned him, such was his solidarity with where we have ended up and with where we have put him.

Moreover, as we know, and as the Church has consistently preached and taught (in what we might now even begin to consider as something more than a story told by simple folk who didn't know any better), Jesus rose from the dead. This is the ultimate sign of what I am calling the victory of the cross. But let's be clear about this: it is not what the first followers of Jesus were expecting. The first Christians were as surprised by the resurrection as we are. Mary Magdalene went to the tomb to anoint a corpse, not greet the dawn of a new age and see a new humanity. But the stone was rolled away. The barriers were broken down. Death itself was conquered and, with it, all the other things that lead to death, particularly all our wrong choices: those things the Church calls sin. They had been defeated. This doesn't mean we no longer see them. We still fail. We still die. But failure and death no longer have a hold on us. There is a new reality and a new hope. It is utterly realistic about the damage that we do to each other and the world, and utterly straightforward about the fact that death comes to each of us. But because Jesus is risen from the dead, these things no longer have the last word. God has spoken a new first word in the resurrection of Jesus, and this is our starting point.

CHAPTER TWELVE

On the first Easter day, Mary Magdalene mistakes the risen Jesus for the gardener. In a way, she is right. He has become what the first Christians called a new Adam, a new first person. The word Adam simply means 'man' or 'human': one made from the earth. The first Adam, the person we read about in those beautiful early chapters of the book of Genesis, represents all of us in our beginnings and in the wrong choices that we make. Jesus is a second Adam. A chance to start again. A new beginning. He is the gardener. He is tending a new creation.

From that point onwards, through Mary Magdalene, St Paul, Polycarp, Bernard of Clairvaux, all those Christian people down through the ages who have popped into my telling of this story, we see who God really is. We see God *through* Jesus.

Those first followers of Jesus reflected on what this meant, both for our life on earth and for a life that is beyond this life: Jesus' resurrection from the dead being the first piece of a new creation.

In the end, the only way they were able to make sense of it was to say that Jesus was himself the Son of God who had been with God from the beginning, and that the Holy Spirit, who they experienced as the continuing and abiding presence of Jesus, was also God. Thus emerged – over several centuries! – this astonishing idea that God is community, what the Church calls the Trinity – three persons, one God.

But seeing God differently also led to seeing humanity differently. There developed a much greater appreciation and understanding that we, too, are made for community: with each other, and with God. And not just with those of our own kind: we are one human household inhabiting one world and with a special and particular responsibility towards each other and towards the world. Moreover, we are at our best when we live in a community.

This has become the Christian understanding: you cannot be yourself on your own. We only find the self-realisation and fulfilment we crave when we enter into these new and transformed relationships that Jesus makes possible.

First of all, with God. This is what is achieved by the uniting of our life with the very life of God in the incarnation of Jesus, the Word. Incarnation is the word the Church uses to describe God becoming human in Jesus. It means literally to 'become enfleshed'. But it happens by God sharing our death as well as our birth.

Second, Jesus makes new relationship with each other possible. He enables us to see each other differently and to stop confining and defining ourselves by all the usual labels and demarcations of race, class, caste, gender and nationality.

We will come on to the new relationship we have with the world in the final chapters, but in another massively important passage in the New Testament, St Paul, the first great architect of Christian thinking, describes how our relationships with each other are transformed by our belonging to Christ in what he calls a 'new humanity'. On more than one occasion he cites three different sets of relationships that are transformed. He says:

in Christ Jesus you are all children of God through faith. As many of you as were baptised into Christ have clothed yourselves with Christ. There is no longer Jew or Greek, there is no longer slave or free, there is no longer male and female; for all of you are one in Christ Jesus. And if you belong to Christ, then you are Abraham's offspring, heirs according to the promise.[1]

It is hard to overstate the significance of these words for Christian thinking about the world. However, it is easy to misconstrue them. Paul is not saying that these distinctions no longer exist. They manifestly do. Rather, he is saying that through baptism – that is, through the Christian sign of belonging (in English culture still popularly called christening) – we enter into a new household where, clothed in Christ, we are one, new humanity. This equality doesn't mean everyone is the same. Male and female, Jew and Greek and, yes, sadly, even slave and free still exist. It is the superiority of one over the other – which was the absolutely accepted status quo of the culture in which Jesus lived – that is now superseded by the new humanity and the new community of the Church, which is the household of those who follow Jesus.

Paul isn't saying that these relationships and differences are being merged or eradicated, but that all relationships and distinctions are taken up into Christ. Paul is describing something fundamental about God. He is describing the beautiful unity in Christ that is not a uniformity.[2]

This was to have huge social and political implications. But it took quite a long while for them to be worked out. We are still doing it. This is a new way of belonging to God and a new way of belonging to each other. The journey towards understanding was to be arduous and perplexing. It still is.

To begin with, Paul is addressing a very real issue: the question of whether Gentile converts to the new way of Christ (it wasn't called Christianity yet) had to be circumcised before they were baptised.

Circumcision was and is basic to Jewish male identity. It is a sign of belonging. It therefore also defined the way that Jewish people related to those around them. Since the first Christians believed that Jesus came to fulfil Judaism, the promise that was made to Abraham – note how Paul makes this connection quite specifically in the passage I've just quoted – is now a promise to everyone. Paul isn't quite saying circumcision doesn't matter any more; he is rejecting the idea that to be uncircumcised is inferior to being circumcised. Therefore, those who are outside Judaism, the recipients of the new universal promises of Christ, don't need to become Jews before they become Christians. What God has done in Jesus has fulfilled Judaism. We no longer need to be constrained by their categories. There is a new unity. Therefore, Gentiles as well as Jews could be baptised into Christ on an equal footing.

This decision, made a few years after the resurrection of Jesus, paved the way for that rapid expansion of the Church across the known world that we explored in a previous chapter: the Christian faith became a worldwide faith operating across a plurality of cultures and religions.

This is very relevant for our situation today. We live in a multi-faith and multi-cultural world. Just as the Christian way could be the fulfilment of Judaism – that is honouring and delighting in everything that the Jewish faith held dear, but going further in the new relationship that God had initiated in Jesus – so it can be the fulfilment of other religions and other philosophies, too. If God is the source and origin of everything that is good, then it follows that God must already be present in all that is good and beautiful in the world. This means that Christians can, at one and the same time, hold to the unique beauty and irreplaceability of God's revelation in Christ *and* honour, respect and delight in the truths about God that are found in other religions and philosophies.

It hasn't always looked that way. Christianity, like other religions and many other philosophies, has been abused and exploited by people who only want to use it as a means of accumulating power for themselves. Sadly, and tragically, this has often meant the Christian faith being pitted against other religions. We have a very bloody history. But at heart, the truths enshrined in the insight that, in Christ, there is no Jew nor Gentile mean we can have a liberatingly different attitude to the religions of the world. We can and do work with people of other faiths and cherish what is good in their traditions. We can continue to tell them about Christ, because we believe that Christ is liberating good news to every person, every philosophy and every faith. But not by sweeping them away: rather, by honouring and fulfilling them.

Furthermore, those of us who do follow Jesus don't really think of Christianity as a religion, or at least not in the same way as other religions. Whereas all the great religions of the world share a belief in the oneness and the holiness of God, only Christianity makes the claim that God has come down to earth. Other religions have prophets who speak clearly and boldly in God's name. Christianity makes the audacious (and to other faiths shocking) claim that Jesus is not just speaking *for* God, Jesus *is* God.

Since we know that in every human culture there is evidence of religion – that is, a system of ordering life so as to have communion with God, seek God's way and even have some kind of access to God – we might define religion as 'the human response to God': something that is naturally present in humanity (how could it be otherwise, since humanity is made in God's image?). But we must, then, also conclude that Christianity is not the same.

Christianity is not the human response to God, but *God's response to humanity*. Therefore, when God is revealed in Jesus – his living *and* his dying – God meets us in our own flesh and blood, creating community with God (a new humanity), which means that religion isn't really needed any more. However, while religions manifestly continue, we are able to speak to them about Jesus and honour the goodness and truth they carry. But one day, all things will be gathered together in Christ. Then it will be clear that we are all – every person and every religion – children of Abraham.

Second, Paul says that in Christ there is no slave or free.

The Christian faith was born into a world where slavery was taken for granted and where many societies were built upon systems of caste and class. All this was seen as normal and taken for granted. Therefore, to say that, in Christ, slaves and free are one – that one is not superior to the other – is about as shocking as you could get. This astonishingly radical and far-reaching statement would change the world. But it took a while. It was so radical and so far-reaching that Paul himself probably couldn't quite realise what it truly meant. After all, it doesn't of itself mean that slavery is abolished, just that slaves and free are one in Christ. However, if they are one in Christ, then there are political implications for how they are treated. And so a long conversation began. As

I mentioned earlier, we can read in one of Paul's other letters how he was starting to work this out: the letter to Philemon is solely dedicated to securing the freedom of a Christian slave.

We also know that because of these radical ideas about a new way of belonging to each other, Christian faith, in those early days, was hugely popular among the poor, the exploited and the excluded. How could it be otherwise? Many lives were restricted and controlled by the bonds of ownership. Human beings had become a merchandise that was bought and sold. The Christian faith offered a different and a unifying narrative about how we belonged together.

But the Christian faith did not simply pit the exploited against the exploiters in adversarial conflict. It sought to transcend differences in a world where slavery was normal. For many centuries this meant treating slaves well rather than opposing slavery. Paul also makes this point in some of his other letters. Therefore, whereas it took only a few years to work out what it meant for Jew or Greek to be one in Christ, it took more than 1,800 years for the Church to really wrestle with what it might mean for there to be no slave or free.

Although at different points in different places throughout history, slavery has been either tolerated or encouraged and sometimes stopped, it was a group of Christians at the end of the eighteenth century who, with others, led the campaign towards a complete end to the practice. It was a hugely significant moment in human history. We were, at last, able to acknowledge to ourselves the fundamental injustice of one human being being owned by another.

But it took a long time. Which means that for hundreds of years faithful Christian people read their Bibles and saw no contradiction in a world that took slavery for granted. In the towns and cities of many wealthy and powerful Western nations, individual families and communities got rich by trafficking slaves. It was a huge multi-million-pound industry. How else were cities like Bristol and Liverpool built? Penny Lane, the street made famous by the Beatles' song, was named after James Penny, a Liverpool merchant who made his money from slavery and who vigorously opposed its abolition.

In Britain, even when slavery was abolished, compensation didn't go to the released slaves, but to the slave owners as recompense for losing their 'property'. Having grown rich on the profits of an obscene trade, slave owners grew richer still from its ending. In fact, the British taxpayer only stopped paying that bill in 2015! The recent Black Lives Matter movement has highlighted the fact that we need to continue to understand the colonial legacy of slavery, the so-called 'race science' that lay behind it and how it made the very idea of slave owning acceptable, and the way these inhuman ideas still cast a shadow across our world, not just in the statues of slave traders in public squares, but in the deeply embedded attitudes about racial superiority that are still only just below the surface of many people and at work in many of the structures of our society.

And slavery itself hasn't been eradicated. Through human trafficking, forced labour, bondage to debt, child domestic slavery and enforced marriage, all sorts of different and invidiously horrible modern slavery still goes on. There are also the near-slave conditions of very poorly paid labourers churning out the cheap clothes and disposable electrical goods that we crave. In some places, all this goes on quite openly. Moreover, we know about it, but do little to change it, still less change our own habits of consumption. It is, sadly, one of the best examples of the fact that left to our own devices, we don't do what is right. We do what is absolutely and grotesquely wrong. It is another example of the complacency and rather foolish optimism of the bankrupt philosophies about human progress and human goodness that simply don't take – and, yes, I'm going to use the word again – human sinfulness seriously.

Moreover, there are other shocking inequalities in our society that are created and exacerbated by white privilege, unconscious bias and, all too often, systemic racism.

While writing this chapter I have been watching the terrible images on the news of George Floyd's murder on the streets of Minneapolis. Even though he was doing nothing to resist detainment, he was secured to the ground by a white American police officer forcibly pressing his knee on his neck. This went on for a painfully shocking eight minutes and forty-six seconds. By the time paramedics arrived, Mr Floyd was dead. His last words were: 'I cannot breathe.'

Understandably, and across the world, this pointlessly evil human act unleashed a howl of frustration and protest from black and minority ethnic people, who from one degree of awfulness to another had experienced similar dehumanising prejudice. Those words, 'I cannot breathe', echoed around the world, summing up so many people's experience of not being given the space to be themselves, of being second-class citizens in someone else's world. This is the antithesis of the belonging and the new humanity the Christian faith declares. But what I use here as a metaphor is for so many people in our world a brutal, daily reality of violent prejudice.

When can we become a world where in Christ there is no black or white? Why is Jesus, a Palestinian Jew, still often portrayed as if he were white? White hegemony still controls the narrative of the world. And white people usually can't see it.

In this regard, racism operates rather like our perception of accent. It is there within us, but we don't acknowledge it. I speak normally, we say to ourselves. Other people have accents.

What is good and hopeful about the Christian faith is that it absolutely confronts the reality of sin: but not with punishment, or an improving lecture about how we must learn to behave better, but with mercy and forgiveness from a God who, in Jesus, takes upon himself the consequences of human failing and kick-starts the ongoing project of building a new humanity, one in which the old distinctions and exclusions don't count, one where prejudice is banished.

No Jew or Greek. No slave or free. And there are others we must add. But now we come to the third distinction Paul mentions: man and woman. Though straightaway, please note the slight, but significant, difference in the language: Jew *or* Greek; slave *or* free; man *and* woman.

The other differences indicate a separation that to one degree or another was a consequence of religious and political difference. In Christ they could find a unity. Man *and* woman speaks of an existing unity that was part of the way humanity had been created, but also confronts the cultural hegemony that had arisen in gender relationships. However, in Christ, male and female will be given a greater unity. These words, therefore, affirm, and at the same time transcend, the very earliest descriptions of humanity where we are made in the image of God *with* our complementarity and difference. One is not superior, or above the other, though we have made it that way. Therefore, in Christ there is a new abundant and strengthened unity.

Working this out, however, remains a work in progress. It took 1,800 years for the world to confront the evil of slavery.

It has taken longer still to challenge the prejudice and inequalities around the inter-relationship between men and women, some of it, of course, bolstered by other passages in the New Testament that do indeed conform to the very power-laden subjugation of women by men that this passage points beyond.

It also indicates that for progress to be made, both women and men need to be liberated.

One of the better stories of the twentieth century is the story of how this has begun, particularly with the emancipation of women. There is still much to be done, not least in the attitudes of many men. In our own society, equality of pay and opportunity still needs to be addressed. In some parts of the world, women are still treated as the belongings of men.

The Church hasn't found this easy. The church I was ordained into had an exclusively male priesthood. There have only been female priests in the Church of England since 1994. We have only had female bishops since 2015. I have lived through this change and seen the tremendous blessing it is when women and men work together as the equal partners God made us to be.

However, nowadays it is impossible to talk about differences of gender and issues of gender equality without also mentioning a whole gamut of other gender- and sexuality-related issues that are unresolved in the Church and not nearly as resolved in society as some would imagine. For the Church, this is a new frontier of prejudice and oppression that we must boldly encounter.

What, for instance, does it mean to live in a church where we can also say that in Christ there is no gay or straight? We are working this one out. We have not yet reached an answer.

This is hugely frustrating for a world where these matters have largely been settled. Even having the debate runs the risk of legitimising some prejudicial views. But Paul's vision of all relationships and all distinctions being taken up into Christ regardless of whether they are those that were there from the beginning in the creation itself (like male and female) or those that are societal and fashioned by our own fallenness (like slave and free) gives us an imaginative framework within which we can honour, and where appropriate accept and embrace, difference.

Consequently, the Church of England has been absolutely clear that all people, regardless of their sexuality, are welcome in the Christian community. We have been absolutely clear that there is no place for homophobia. What we are still working out is not whether LGBTI+ people are welcome or not. They are. We are working out what is the appropriate way of acknowledging and giving expression to that welcome. We can do this because we are absolutely clear that every person is made in the image of God, and that in Christ all people are brought together into a new humanity.

These groups of people are rarely mentioned in the Bible. Even when they are, the texts themselves require careful examination lest we muddle up the categories of one age with those of another (as with the debate over slavery and gender). But the controlling idea, which is so relevant for all our relationships and for the way we order the world, is that in Christ we are a new humanity: we are one. In this new humanity, difference is not eradicated, it is included, and one is not inferior to the other.

Therefore, these words of Paul echo down the centuries, provoking and challenging us to look ever more closely at the way we see each other, the way we treat each other, and the way we learn to examine our own unconscious bias and the presuppositions that have shaped us, allowing us to treat others as different and separate. They teach us that unity is not uniformity, that difference is not a threat.

In the story of the coming of the Holy Spirit, the disciples all speak in different languages so that every person in Jerusalem is able to hear them in their mother tongue. This, too, is a sign of God's celebration of difference. Being one in Christ, therefore, is not to speak some holy Esperanto. The difference between different nations and cultures is not a threat to unity and community. God uses them to build the rainbow nation that is the Church of Jesus Christ.

Part of our belonging to the Christian community is to learn to live as 'resident aliens' in our communities in the way that Mathetes described to Diognetus all those years ago. We are called to transcend, and not to be tied down by or defined by, the ideas and conventions with which we were brought up. There is a new beginning.

Or to put it another way: our hearts are changed. That heart which was full of wilful pride, of mistrust or prejudice, is taken away. God gives us a new heart: the heart of Jesus Christ. We become part of a new humanity.

And that's where I ended up at Paddington Station.

In the couple of minutes we had when that young woman asked me why I was a priest, I told her that it was because I believed in God, that I believed that God was made known in Jesus, that I believed God wanted, through Jesus and through me, to change the world and that God was going to do it by changing my heart.

And that is where I have now – at last! – ended up with you, dear England.

I didn't get round to saying that God could change her

heart as well. Though I believe God can. She, after all, had some interesting things to say to me – and we will return to them shortly.

But God's love is a totality. It is an equal and ever-replenishing distribution of unconditional affirmation and grace. It is for her as much as for me. It is for you, too.

Nor was I able to say all the things I've now said to you.

I don't know whether they would have made much difference. When I did get to that symposium in Wales and told people about my encounter for the first time, some said I should have missed the train; I should have stayed and carried on the conversation. But I'm not sure that's right. No one believes because of the power of someone else's persuasion. Eloquent rhetoric is rarely a reliable barometer of truth. And even if they did, someone else will come along tomorrow with another set of ideas to persuade them otherwise: tyrants, snake-oil salesmen and silver-tongued manipulators are two a penny. They always have been. They are not to be trusted. Especially the religious ones, who tell you that the Christian faith is a deal and you must sign on the dotted line. It is not. It is a declaration of love. And, therefore, it is absolutely free. Free to receive. And free to decline.

Therefore, all my words then, and all my words now, can only help you to pause and find your *own* words and your *own* response to the strange and beautiful story of Jesus. They are not meant to be more or less than this. All I hope is that maybe I've cleared some of the obstacles out of the way, and that you can at least see Jesus clearly and make up your own mind.

So as you turn over the page to the final chapters in the last part of this letter, I am simply going to dream with you about what our dear country might become if we inhabited it differently. I hope we will still live in close relationship with Ireland, Scotland and Wales and in a renewed relationship with Europe, distinct, but not separate. But what will that look like? How are we called to be part of the story?

I believe our best future will emerge when we learn how we belong to each other and how we can build communities of belonging.

So these next chapters are going to be unapologetically hopeful. How could it be otherwise when I see what God has done for me in Jesus Christ? How he loves me and has changed my heart. In him I have found hope. God has given me a new heart.

Part Three

CHANGING THE WORLD

CHAPTER THIRTEEN

Dear England,

In delightful contrast to those ways of understanding self that begin and end with self, I think it was Bishop Michael Marshall who said, 'I worship, therefore I am.'

He was expressing the Christian truth that is at the heart of this letter: that you cannot be yourself on your own! That true and lasting joy is found elsewhere.

You need others and you need God. It is not that life will be miserable or without meaning without God and without others, but it's not what was intended. We are made for community. As Bernard of Clairvaux insisted all those centuries ago, a true love of self is found in relationship with God. We become ourselves in relationship with others. This has huge implications.

I am not, as the world often seems to insist, an isolated, self-actualising individual around whom the world turns. Happiness and fulfilment will not be found by accumulating wealth and privilege, not even through health, not even through human rights and freedoms. They may be enormously beneficial, but of themselves they cannot deliver what they presume to promise. Moreover, because some of them – for example, access to healthcare in many parts of the world – are limited, part of the allure of wealth is the access it brings to things that others don't have. Therefore, tragically, even wanting these things can drive a wedge between you and your neighbour, not bring you together. In fact, in so much of the liberal, free-market economy that we live in, competition with each other for limited resources only unleashes those selfish and ultimately self-destructive passions that lurk within each of us. Seeking the 'common good' easily becomes a luxury only to be considered when my 'own good' is properly secured first. And that day never quite comes. I could always do with a bit more.

The way of Christ offers something different. My own good can only be secured by securing the common good of all. I do not exist in isolation: not as an individual person, not as a family, not as a tribe, not even as a nation. As we will go on to consider, it is not that these belongings are wrong (they can in fact be the glue of good community), but each of them needs to be liberated from the fearful, inward pressure to keep others out. For however high I build the walls around me, the world – and others – will still get in.

There has to be another way. This is the way we see in Christ: his expansive vision of a new humanity. Moreover, and this is something all the great spiritual writers have insisted on down through the centuries, the one thing you can never get away from is yourself. Even in glorious, pampered and privileged isolation you will still have to confront your own fears, your own regrets and disappointments, not least the nagging self-doubt that your success in carving out a space for yourself has cut you off not only from others but also from all the possibilities of love that you know can only blossom when you let others in. Therefore, the first thing to do is to make peace with yourself. You need to accept your own failings, vulnerabilities and needs. In order to embrace love, you must be open to the likelihood of hurt.

Those who can't cry often can't laugh either. And here comes the paradox of Christian faith: you gain yourself by losing yourself.

The Christian virtues of self-control and self-restraint, and from them a whole other way of inhabiting the world in which we love our neighbour as our self, arise from an attitude to self that is rooted in Jesus' injunction that if anyone wants to save their life, they must lose it. What does this mean?

First, and counterintuitively for a consumer society in which I am forever supposed to be satisfying the hungers within, it means that I cannot find happiness and fulfilment on my own and from within myself. I can only find it in relationship with God and, through God, with others. I can only find it by recognising my *creatureliness*, that is, that I am created by God and part of God's big, beautiful 'making love possible' creation. My destiny and the destiny of the whole creation is bound up with God, and therefore bound up with others and with the creation itself. Losing yourself doesn't mean getting lost, but being found by something bigger, something with which 'yourself' makes sense as part of the whole.

What I am losing is my inbuilt tendency to put myself first. I am losing my insistence that my well-being matters more than others'. I am losing that way of ordering the world where there is a hierarchy of need (with mine at the top). And to have my life saved is to recognise that I cannot save myself, that I need that power which is outside myself, which, it turns out, is love itself, the source and mirror of the most powerful force within me. This God who is love knows what it's like to be myself, knows me better than I know myself and still loves me. This God sets me free from the conse-quences of all my wrong choices (and the desire to repeat them). All this is the work of God in Jesus Christ. The fruit of it – or what you might call the cash value in the life I lead each day – is that I have a new relationship with myself.

It leads to things like self-control and self-restraint, things that in an older, classical tradition were seen as necessary for the good ordering of society, but are now thought to be old-fashioned, or just impossibly idealistic.

Why would anyone deny themselves? Well, the Christian answer is because ultimately it is in your own best interest! Your self-denial, and the self-discipline required for self-denial, will contribute to a world of self-denial and therefore to a world of mutual giving. It is also the way that love becomes a possibility. Freedom, in this new humanity, is not freedom to do as I like provided it doesn't hurt anyone, but freedom *from* the things that harm me and the things that prevent me from becoming who I am meant to be. The chains of hedonistic and hubristic selfhood are unshackled. I lose them, and I find myself in Christ. There is a picture in God's heart of this beautiful person I am capable of becoming with this new freedom. I discover that God has a purpose for my life.

God does want to change me, but not into someone else (which, on reflection, seems to be the message of the world, forever trying to sell me a highly idealised version of what humanity could be if, clambering over the backs of others, I were the one with the fast car and the beautiful body). God wants to change me into something of more lasting beauty: the person I am meant to be.

The world offers the illusion that if my bank balance changed, I might be happy and fulfilled. God works on the heart. Hence, if I had to offer a soundbite for the Christian faith, it would be this: *in Christ you can become yourself*. This new selfhood steers us into new and exciting places.

The political consequences of this are that the privileging of personal choice as a good that trumps many others should no longer have such a deciding vote in the way we order society. Ironically, it is the coronavirus pandemic that has reminded us of this. Writing, as I am, from the midst of the lockdown, we have all seen our personal choices massively curtailed. Pubs, restaurants, clubs, theatres, gyms, even church buildings are all closed. We have even had to give up each other. Conversations, if they happen at all, take place from a two-metre distance. This has been really hard, not least for the economy. But we have all accepted the importance of self-denial. We are losing ourselves so as to find ourselves. It is what Graham Tomlin has called 'a crash course in a new moral universe'.[1] But its lessons must last.

So let's look at this in relation to four areas of our lives: family; community; nation; and world. These are all areas that require a change of heart.

We start with family.

Despite the difficult and indeed the unspeakably horrid and abusive experiences that some people have, the family remains the basic building block of society.

The latest statistics show that there are 27.2 million households in the UK and that the average household size is 2.4 persons. Of these, there are 19 million families, family here meaning a married, civil-partnered or cohabiting couple with or without children, or a lone parent with at least one child.[2] That is a lot of people living together with some sort of commitment to each other. It doesn't mean that the household units are stable or permanent. But many are. To have a family or be part of a family, or even to just be happily married within a stable and lasting relationship, remains the heartfelt wish of many people.

This still means that just under 4 million people between sixteen and twenty-four are living alone. Then, of course, there are another 3.8 million people over sixty-five who live alone, many of them widows or widowers. But those who live alone, even out of choice, still cherish the wider network of their family. To take family seriously does not mean disparaging those who choose to be single. In Christ there is no married or single. One is not better than the other. But most people do choose to live with someone else and to have a family. For most of us, being part of a family is the greatest source of joy and affirmation. It is where we learn what love looks like and feels like, its joys and its responsibilities. Though, as with anything of value, there is also regret and frustration along the way.

Those who love us and give us the most affirmation are also the ones who are unflinchingly honest with us. This can be painful.

Most of us are also aware that we haven't given those we love the time, energy and affirmation they needed in return. As the tired, but nevertheless accurate, cliché has it: no one's tombstone declares they wished they'd spent more time at the office! Our family are the people we want to be with. Our children are the ones for whom we would lay down our lives.

Therefore, family should be taken much more seriously in our political debate. But apart from some helpful tax incentives, family is not often spoken about. We don't think of the family as the school for love and the school for good citizenship that it must become, and usually is. This of course doesn't mean that we don't carry on saving people, especially abused children and women, from degrading and exploitative families. But we recognise that most families, thank God, are not like this. Most families are places of safety and nurture, where we learn how to live. Therefore, our political debate and the policies that shape our national life should pass the test of whether they are supporting and encouraging family life, making families safe, and at the same time not demeaning those who don't live in families.

In the Jewish tradition out of which the Christian faith grew, family was basic to human society and human flourishing, though the family then was not the small nuclear family that we tend to think of – Mum and Dad and 2.2 children. In fact, the word that is used in the Bible isn't really family at all, but *household*.

Dating back to those times when the Hebrew people led a nomadic life, the word household describes a wider network of people, including grandparents, uncles, aunts, cousins and, no doubt, a few other hangers-on who had been acquired along the way. It would have included those who were single as well as those who were married. Together, with their goods and their animals, these people formed a household. It is what communities and nations are made of. A household is both a microcosm of society and a model for how human beings should live together.

This then is a challenge to the Christian Church as well as to society. The Church needs to expand its understanding of family, recognising that the concept of household is richer, broader and more inclusive. It is better able to celebrate difference. Such a conceptual shift might help us learn how to include those whose lifestyles and predispositions challenge what has been the norm for a long time, but may not reflect the new humanity we have in Christ where difference is looked at, well, differently.

Furthermore, during exile when their country had been

over-run and they had been carried off into captivity, the Jewish people held their faith and identity together by making the home the centre of their lives. Stripped of all that had appeared to be essential to their faith, losing even the temple itself that had been so central to their life and worship, they put themselves back together in their homes by developing a whole way of life that was shaped by their belief in God and the values that sprang from those beliefs. We in the Church may benefit from a similar re-education.

It is another irony of the coronavirus pandemic that we have been exiled in our homes. For those whose homes are frightening and dangerous, this has been a horror but, again, for most of us it has been an education. In my own family, with two of my grown-up sons locked down with me, we have rediscovered some of the rhythms and patterns of family life that were there many years ago when they were younger, but have been lost along the way, not just because they'd left home, but because of the frantic busyness of the lives we were leading. So, for a few months, we again found ourselves eating a meal together each day (as well as taking it in turns to cook). This was a revelation and a gift. Fellowship around the dinner table is the glue of family life. Yet, I'm told that many of the houses on our burgeoning new estates – houses that are penny-pinching in terms of space, anyway – do not even have a dining room. Somehow we have let go of the idea that sitting together and eating a meal might be a good thing. Once there was a room dedicated to it. Now we sit in front of our separate television sets (or tablets) in our separate rooms eating separate meals, and therefore, even under the same roof, leading separate lives. One of the first great revolutions we could make is eating together.

Furthermore, in the Christian faith, as with the Jewish

faith, a meal is at the heart of our worship. In the Christian Church, the Eucharist, the great remembrance of deliverance from sin and death, happens in a church building. But in Judaism, the Passover meal, the great remembrance of deliverance from slavery, happens in the home. During the coronavirus pandemic many churches have been streaming services and many people who weren't regular church attenders have been joining in. And many Christian people have rediscovered a worshipping life in the home.

This is a wonderful thing. One of the ways in which we shall ensure that our hearts are aligned with God's purposes and that we are part of God's plans to change the world is by praying. And although prayer is hard to define, it is easy to begin.

Prayer is not trying to tune into an elusive wavelength called God. Prayer is opening up your heart and mind to God and letting God fill you with God's love. Moreover, prayer is not about bending God's ear or trying to change God's mind, but about allowing your will and your agenda to be shaped by God's will and God's agenda. It is the actual expression of that relationship with God and with others that is the source and sustenance of our humanity, the way in which we become truly ourselves and find where true joy is available. Prayer is not our demand for God's intervention, but our willing collaboration. In communion and community with God, we are changed.

Simple prayers in the home – giving thanks each morning for the gift of life and the gift of a new day, dedicating that day to living in such a way that your life contributes to the well-being of the world, giving thanks before each meal for the basic provisions needed to live each day, and reminding yourself of the millions who have neither enough to eat, nor warmth, shelter, access to healthcare, nor many of the things that we too easily take for granted, giving time for reflection and contemplation that our minds and wills are shaped by God – can be offered just as easily as you walk the dog as by sitting in rapt silence! Subsequently, at the end of each day, reviewing what has been and being prepared to say sorry for what should not have been: all this makes a difference. All of it can be nurtured in the home.

'To clasp the hands in prayer is the beginning of an uprising against the disorder of the world', said the great Swiss theologian, Karl Barth.[3] As we make space for God to work in us, especially in our homes as they are expanded into households, so the whole ordering of the world changes.

CHAPTER FOURTEEN

The word economy comes from two Greek words: *oikos*, meaning household – the very word that builds on and expands our understanding of family that we have just been talking about – and *nomos*, meaning law. So the literal meaning is 'the law of the household'. Furthermore, *nomos* is from another Greek word, *nemein*, meaning to distribute, indicating that law and justice here have something to do with fair distribution.

This seems to me to be a good place to begin thinking about a Christian perspective on the economic life of communities, regions and nations. A good economy is meant to be like a well-run household.[1] And funnily enough, even though most of us do not claim a great understanding of economics (and I sometimes think that economists and the politicians they advise would prefer to keep it that way), we do know what a well-run household should be like. One of the things we take for granted – in fact, if it wasn't there we would hold up our hands in horror – is that everyone is catered for according to their need. There is no preferential treatment. Everyone is treated equally and fairly. In a family – a household – it would be unthinkable that at the dinner table some were fed while others went hungry.

This approach to life – and economics – is sometimes called distributive justice. It is a theme that runs through the Bible, especially the prophets of the Old Testament who, if you ever find yourself getting round to reading them, rage against the people of Israel, saying that what God wants is not their worship and their festivals, but justice.

Let me give you just a couple of searing examples. The language is as rich as any knockabout exchange in the House of Commons at PMQs:

I hate, I despise your festivals . . .
Even though you offer me your burnt-offerings and grain-
    offerings,
        I will not accept them;
and the offerings of well-being of your fatted animals
        I will not look upon.
Take away from me the noise of your songs;
        I will not listen to the melody of your harps.
But let justice roll down like waters,
        and righteousness like an ever-flowing stream.[2]

Or:

. . . bringing offerings is futile;
        incense is an abomination to me . . .
Your new moons and your appointed festivals
        my soul hates;
        they have become a burden to me,
        I am weary of bearing them.
When you stretch out your hands,
        I will hide my eyes from you;
even though you make many prayers,
        I will not listen;
        your hands are full of blood.

Wash yourselves; make yourselves clean;
> remove the evil of your doings
> from before my eyes;
cease to do evil,
> learn to do good;
seek justice,
> rescue the oppressed,
defend the orphan,
> plead for the widow.[3]

What God wants is justice, the justice that can only come when we recognise that we inhabit this planet together with mutual responsibility to one another and to the land itself.

In the book of Psalms, which is the great prayer book of the Bible, we learn that God's very nature is justice and mercy. Psalm 89 says that 'righteousness and justice are the foundation of [God's] throne'.[4] Psalm 99 says that God is a 'lover of justice' who has 'established equity' and 'executed justice'.[5]

But we don't always think about justice as the means by which everything is distributed fairly. The reason the prophets are so enraged is because of the injustices they see around them. In turning their back on God, the people have also turned their backs on the righteous ways of God. So it is that widows and orphans are neglected and strangers are ignored or exploited. Because the people of Israel had been slaves themselves in Egypt, this lack of concern to those who are aliens in their midst is a particular affront to God's justice. Another of the prophets makes it clear: what God requires of us is that we do justice, love kindness and walk humbly with God.[6]

In popular parlance, when people speak about seeking justice, they often just mean seeking retribution. God's vision is much bigger and much more positive. Even where some form of retribution is necessary and appropriate, this is only one form of justice among many others. What we need is a similarly expansive vision of justice, community and wholeness.

Arising from its Jewish roots, the Christian tradition has always believed that to be just, as God is just, means to distribute everything fairly. When the people of Israel were liberated from slavery in Egypt and were wandering in the desert, God fed them with manna from heaven. Everyone had enough. But no one had more than enough. And, because they had been slaves themselves, the good stewardship of the household of God's earth extended to others, especially those who were strangers, aliens and outcasts. The Jewish faith developed a beautiful and complex system of Sabbath rest and jubilee whereby every year a portion of the harvest was left for the 'poor and for the alien',[7] and every seventh year the land itself should rest 'so that the poor of your people may eat'.[8] And every fiftieth year, that is after 'seven times seven' years, there was a kind of super-Sabbath for the land, when not only did the land rest, but debts were cancelled and the land returned to its original owners. The reason? '[T]he land is mine,' says God, 'with me you are but aliens and tenants.'[9]

This adds a new dimension to our stewardship. God requires us to share what we have with those who are in need, not just because the people of Israel had been slaves themselves, but because all of us, the whole human household, are aliens and tenants. We do not own the land. We must treat it fairly, preserve its fertility and share its goodness. Sabbath rest, it turns out, is not just a useful reminder that mindfulness is good for us and has been around for quite a while, but a political act: an injunction to good and just stewardship of the world where rest and equitable distribution follow the pattern that God initiates in the creation itself and that mirrors the reciprocity and generosity that exists within the Godhead. The first disciples, whose whole religious world-view, like that of Jesus himself, grew out of this tradition, also held all things in common.[10] Their life and witness was not just a private matter; their trust and confidence in Jesus and the Jewish faith that he was steeped in had given birth to a whole set of ideas and a way of inhabiting the earth. Therefore, from a Christian perspective, in all areas of life, fair distribution and the good stewardship that allows the earth itself to breathe and rest and maintain its fertile goodness seems to be the yardstick: fair distribution of food; fair distribution of security; fair distribution of land and education, access to health and opportunity, even access to the means of justice itself. So even if such justice requires retribution or punishment, it is done fairly.

In the years leading up to our debates about Brexit and then the horrors of the coronavirus pandemic, we have witnessed a drawing back of the state. Both in national and local government, we have become less likely to think of the state or government as being responsible for ensuring these things are distributed fairly. Instead, the market ruled. Wealth, we were told, would trickle down. People would be responsible for themselves.

Personal responsibility and enterprise are good things. They are to be encouraged. But in a household, they won't be separate from mutual responsibility and support for the weak, the elderly and the infirm. However, our ideas about society have changed. We are much more likely to think of ourselves as a collection of individuals rather than as a household. Therefore, the vision of the post-war welfare state in which everyone received, for instance, equal access to health regardless of their means and according to their need, started to look more and more like a safety net for those who weren't able to pay for the private medicine that would have pushed them up the queue. Indeed, parts of the overall healthcare provision began to be franchised out to companies whose motivation was as much profit for their shareholders as delivery of a just and equitable service. This is not necessarily wrong in itself. But it is one of the reasons that, when the pandemic came, we were under-prepared compared to some countries. It is better for the bottom line *not* to stockpile PPE. Even access to law, one of the bedrock principles of a democracy, started to look like something only certain people could afford.

The vision that we belonged to each other and were glad to share responsibility for each other rested upon a shared sense of identity as a nation and a people. Strengthened through the crisis of warfare, it sustained us for quite a time. However, it is that very sense of who we are that has changed. It has already cut our ties with Europe, and as I write it remains unclear what the consequences of that decision will actually be. As border controls are established between Britain and Northern Ireland, and as the Scots who didn't vote for Brexit press for another referendum on their own independence, it threatens the internal unity of the United Kingdom itself. In particular, this is having a very damaging impact on the lives of those for whom wealth and opportunity has not trickled down.

For the first time in ages we have seen the gap between rich and poor increasing. Even before the coronavirus pandemic, the Resolution Foundation think tank said that the wealth gap had opened up between 2016 and 2018: the wealth of the top 10 per cent of the population increased by 11 per cent whereas the bottom 10 per cent's increased by just 3 per cent.[11] Regional variations are even more stark. Household wealth in the south-east was found to be more than twice as high as in the north-east. Child poverty is also on the rise. The Children's Society reckons that four million children live in poverty. That's a third of all children living in the UK, the equivalent of nine children in an average classroom. The measure for poverty they use is a child living in a family whose income is below 60 per cent of the UK's average after adjusting for family size. Even if you disagree with this measure, you are still left with a shockingly inequitable distribution of income and opportunity. It means, for instance, that there are couples in the UK living with two children and having less than £58 per day to live on: that's slightly less than £15 per person. So, after housing costs, which for such a family would usually be paid by other benefits, there is £15 per person per day for food, clothes, bills, transport, childcare if you need it, let alone school trips and other activities that more wealthy families take for granted.[12] No wonder foodbanks have become such a feature of contemporary Britain. It is a terrible indictment of our common failures to live fairly with one another. But with such poverty, other things diminish as well, health and education being the most damaging.

Neither has Covid-19 been the great leveller some people imagined. It has affected poorer areas and the BAME community disproportionately, because these are the people – our fellow citizens and neighbours – who are most likely to live in the most cramped conditions, on the lowest incomes, and therefore most likely to have more underlying health conditions, and less ability to stay at home or work from home or social distance. Like many other social advantages, social isolation turned out to be an economic luxury that only the wealthy could really afford.

Furthermore, while Covid-19 hit the health of the elderly, it hit the wealth of the young. We have seen in the past that when you come into the labour market during a financial crisis you are on a lower earning trajectory for decades. This is just one of a number of uncomfortable realities we are having to face up to. High unemployment is another. This has had another damaging impact. For generations there has been a sort of unwritten inter-generational contract: parents expected their children to do better than them, to earn more and to have access to greater opportunities. That progress now seems to have gone into reverse. This is bad in itself, but it will also have unforeseen consequences on the way this generation of young people feels about the society they live in. And if it means they feel less inclined to support it, less confident that they are cared for, less able to achieve, then the consequences could be very damaging indeed. This is more than economic pessimism in the usual way we use the word 'economy'. It is feeling that you are outside the household altogether, that you no longer have a place. It will further separate us from one another, and further loosen the bonds that could bind us together, and will further obscure the vision of our belonging to each other that, I believe, is the best way of moving forward into a fairer future.

My argument is this: just as a good household, a good family, looks after all its members and would not consider doing otherwise – indeed, would happily make the sacrifices that are necessary to ensure that the weakest and most vulnerable are not left out – so should a good society. But as a society we don't seem to be prepared to live out the same principles of generosity, sacrifice and responsibility that we embrace in our families.

Paradoxically, this is also an area where the poor themselves may lead us. Both in this country and around the world, I have always been humbled and amazed by the sacrifices I see some of the poorest people make on behalf of one another and in the service of a greater good. Often the wealthier you are, the more insulated your life becomes, leaving you less able to see a different way of living, or even notice the harm your more isolated lifestyle is doing, not least to yourself. So, for instance, I remember a visit I made to South Africa some years ago, when I was working in the diocese of Oxford. We were twinned with the diocese of Kimberley and Kuruman, and I was making my first ever visit to Africa. I was staying with the archdeacon and parish priest of Upington near the Namibian border. I wrote to him and said that in England when visitors came to us from overseas, we often put them up in the homes of parishioners: would it be possible for me to do the same when I came to him? I didn't really know what I was asking. Most of the parish is the township of Paballelo. When I got to Upington, I did indeed spend most of the time staying in the vicarage with the parish priest and his wife. But I also stayed a couple of nights with one of his parishioners. Receiving hospitality from some of the poorest people in the world was one of life's most moving and powerful experiences: from their scarcity they shared with me everything they had abundantly. I stayed with Maria and her two daughters. Their little corrugated-iron shack was divided into four spaces. There was no running water in the house. There was no toilet. There was only one proper bed. This was given to me. Maria and her daughters somehow slept in one of the other spaces. As I went to sleep on that first night, hearing the sounds of the township, and looking through the holes in the roof at the stars, I felt completely disconnected from everything that I had grown up with and taken for granted, and at the same time more deeply connected than I think I had ever been before with that which is most basic about our humanity.

Very early in the morning, through the 'not much more than cardboard' wall that separated me from Maria and her daughters, I heard her rise and pray. For ten or fifteen minutes she offered prayers of thanksgiving and intercession to God. She dedicated the day to God's service. Half an hour later, she tapped on my door and brought me a cup of tea and a basin of hot water so that I could wash. While I had carried on dozing, she had been outside lighting a fire, preparing breakfast and providing for my needs.

Soon her daughters were ready for school. Dressed immaculately, they set off on the long walk they took each day. Neighbours from surrounding homes gathered with us. Maria's household was one among other households where people worked together, shared what they had and looked out for one another.

It was not a perfect society. Of course it wasn't. There was crime and there were drugs and there was violence. But what there wasn't was separation. And this bred a powerful hopefulness. I have seen it elsewhere.

Last year, I saw it in northern Kenya visiting the diocese of Marsabit, where, at the time, they had not had any proper rain for eighteen months. Many of their animals were already dying, and the fear was that the people would die next. Visiting a village with the local bishop, the elders and parish priest showed me their empty water hole.

Most of us will have seen things like this on the television over the years. Often, we have become immune to them. Seeing the devastation of drought and the famine that quickly follows first-hand was not only hugely distressing, it brought home to me the shattering impact of climate change on the poorest communities in the world. But it was also a lesson in human community and hopefulness. Once again, this community that had so little welcomed me as their guest and shared with me what they had.

And as I remember the astonishing hospitality of these people, my mind also turns to some of our poorest and most deprived communities in this country, where I have witnessed and received incredible generosity. I'm thinking of Blanche, a parishioner in the south London parish where I was a curate: she had lived through and experienced the horrors of two world wars, had lost many loved ones along the way, and was now elderly, ill and housebound in her little council flat on the fourth floor. Yet she was the hub of a network of prayer, generosity and mutual support that was helping to sustain many people who were not only struggling to make ends meet, but also carried all kinds of scars and faced many challenges each day. I visited her often. She was hardly ever alone. The single mum from downstairs or the teenager who was going off the rails were often to be found with her. And if they weren't there, she was praying for them. She had a gift for making community. It arose from her own community with God. Even though it had been broken many times along the way, her heart had been changed and was now changing others.

Let me say again: I am not suggesting that people with wealth and security are unable to live this way. I could give many examples of those who have used their wealth and influence to change the world for the better. Similarly, there are too many poor people in the world. Often their lives have been so broken by poverty and lack of opportunity that, having been knocked down so many times, the only response left is to fight back. But the danger of wealth, when unchecked and unconditioned, is that it cocoons you from your neighbour, breeds a dangerous self-sufficiency and with it a vacuous superiority. If there is no compelling vision of what it means to be human beyond the security of self, we build a world of terrible, selfish isolation.

There is nothing good about poverty. But, equally, there is nothing good about wealth if it is not shared. We need wealth in order to work for the eradication of poverty. But more than anything, we need vision.

Consequently, the things that we can learn about God's good ordering of the world will and must affect our families and our local communities, but they may also lead us to think about the nation-state in a new way and about the sort of communities we need to build.

Having been told for years that expensive government intervention was neither feasible, affordable nor desirable, and that the marketplace could deliver solutions for the world's problems, there have been two occasions in little more than a decade – the banking crisis of 2008–10 and now the coronavirus pandemic – where the state has come to the rescue. With Covid-19, the governments of the world spent literally trillions in a few days. We had been told that magic money trees didn't exist. A whole forest of them was quickly discovered, chopped down and spent. This dramatic change in economic policy may, or may not, lead to a broader public acceptance of a larger and more interventionist government: it certainly goes against the grain of most public thinking from Margaret Thatcher onwards. But it does mean we have an opportunity for, throughout history, crises and disasters have been the catalysts for change. Indeed, it was in 2008, just days after Barack Obama's election, and in the first anxious convulsions of the financial crisis, that his chief of staff, Rahm Emanuel, famously said: 'You never want to waste a serious crisis.'[13]

Sometimes the changes that have come out of a crisis have been for the better: the global flu epidemic of 1918 helped create national health services in many European countries; and the Great Depression of the 1930s and then the Second World War created the impetus for the modern welfare state.

Sometimes the change has been less encouraging. Shoshana Zuboff has named our times the age of surveillance,[14] and she dates its start to the terrorist attacks of 9/11 when the US government's concerns over the internet shifted from how to regulate those who were violating hard-won privacy norms and rights to how these same companies can collect data for them. Consequently, internet surveillance increased hugely. Moreover, without regulation, other disorders took root in our society, not least the ubiquitous (and highly effective) shopping algorithms that are the very best evidence that someone is watching you.

In the modern economy it has been said that data is the new oil. We are being mined.

In the UK, that same financial crisis of 2008 was paid for by the public. Public services were slashed. Austerity policies commenced. These disproportionately hit the poorest in society, leading to the escalating need we see around us in the UK: more homeless people on our streets; more children in poverty; more foodbanks. These are things the Church deals with on a daily basis in the care and service we offer, alongside others, to our local communities. As I have already intimated, it also left us less well prepared than others to meet the sudden onslaught of a major health crisis.

We mustn't make these mistakes again. Learning from the optimism of previous generations, we must build a different sort of world. And the principles upon which we build should be those we find at the heart of God and in God's good ordering of the world: a reciprocity of love and mutual giving that is embodied in those ideas about the economy being like a good household; and the good stewardship of the earth, recognising that it does not belong to us but that we are its stewards. Bolstered by God's great desire for human flourishing, a different way is possible.

CHAPTER FIFTEEN

During the first lockdown of the coronavirus pandemic most of us stood in the streets on Thursday evenings and clapped for the NHS. It was a powerful and moving expression of solidarity with a group of men and women whose service to the nation we all had fresh reasons to be thankful for. Covid-19's invisible and invidious intrusion into our lives meant that we were all keenly aware of our own frailty and mortality. With it we were thankful for those who put their own lives at risk each day to be there for us if – God forbid – we contracted Covid-19 too.

As the days went by our appreciation expanded. Suddenly, we were aware not just of the sacrifice and skill of nurses and doctors, but also of hospital porters and cleaners. Even hospital managers, those 'pen-pushers' and 'arrangers of red tape' that successive governments had said we could do without, suddenly came into their own. Procuring the equipment that was needed, rearranging schedules, and with the help of the armed forces even establishing whole new hospitals, they were the ones who succeeded where so often government failed.

The story of how the Nightingale Hospital in east London came into being is truly inspiring, reminding us of what we can achieve with will and ingenuity. On 21 and 22 March, military planners and staff from NHS England visited the Excel Exhibition and Convention Centre in

Newham for the first time. On 24 March, the Health Secretary announced plans to establish a new hospital there. On 3 April, the facility was formally opened by the Prince of Wales (via a video link). On 7 April, the first patients were admitted.

But our praise went further still. As we withdrew into the lockdown of isolation and social distancing, so we came to appreciate all those other people whose work and service enabled us to live: police officers, delivery drivers, and those who stacked supermarket shelves in the middle of the night. Moreover, some of those whom we were relying on every day, such as delivery drivers, were on a zero-hours contract with virtually no job or financial security and probably very little choice about having to work. The social care system that was now stretched to breaking point and where so many people needlessly died was absolutely dependent on low-paid workers and staffing resources that had for decades been under-invested in. Local councils were often working heroically to keep things going, but with very little resource. It felt like a whole re-education in whose work really mattered, upending the snobbery and indifference of a society that took too many people for granted and disproportionately rewarded those whose labour – so it turned out – wasn't necessarily as essential as we thought. Of course this isn't really the point. It's not that we reverse our priorities. Rather, that we create a level playing field.

Furthermore, be they economic migrants from Eastern Europe and the Middle East, or second- or third-generation Black British, many of the people whose work we were now appreciating were from a black, Asian or minority ethnic background. Especially in the health service. But in other important industries as well. In the summer of 2020, fruit needed picking, but the workers from overseas, the very people whose presence and contribution had been such a political football during the Brexit debates, were no longer available. In that same summer, the killing of George Floyd in Minnesota and the Black Lives Matter movement again challenged us to see ourselves differently, and, for those of us who are white, to face up to the ways our privilege has contorted the world. Everyone needs air to breathe.

The damage to our economy is very real. Its demise is also suffocating. Many are suffering as a result. The decline in GDP in 2020 was the largest since the Second World War. We need it to grow again, but not just in the service of a few, nor at the expense of the many, and certainly not at the expense of the planet itself. In order for a household to prosper, we need those who will create the wealth but we also need those who support them in a hundred different ways and whose labour is just as important and whose humanity is the same. Once again, we find ourselves needing a new normal. Our wealth creators and entrepreneurs need to be back at work. But we also need a skilled and willing workforce, people who are motivated and able to do the work that has to be done for the household of the nation to function and thrive, and we need a new determination to reward people according to their need, not simply according to their financial productivity.

Or, to put it another way: even though our appreciation of the National Health Service may have grown recently, it isn't really new. This has long been a very cherished part of our national life and what is strange is that we don't apply the same criteria to all the other things we need in order for the household of the whole nation to run well: like education, law, and those other necessities and utilities that we rely on. We must, therefore, stop thinking of the NHS as an *exception* in British life: everything else that does not immediately create financial wealth has its funding stripped away, but the NHS carries on. The way we fund and support the NHS could be the model for a new normal, embodying a set of ideas and principles about mutuality, generosity and sacrifice that can be nurtured in other institutions. Together they can lead us to a new way of inhabiting the world.

Interestingly, in the Greek in which the New Testament was written, there isn't a separate word for 'health' and 'salvation' (salvation is the word Christians use to describe what God has done in Jesus in 'saving' us from ourselves and from sin and death and creating a new world order). They are the same Greek word *sozo*. So when, famously, Jesus says, in John 3:17, that 'God did not send the Son into the world to condemn the world, but in order that the world might be saved through him', the words '*saved* through him' could just as accurately be translated as 'have *health* through him'.

The New Testament worldview does not make distinctions between 'mind', 'body' and 'spirit' in the way we do. This is rooted in the Hebrew concept of *shalom*, a word we translate as 'peace', but that is, again, much deeper and broader than this. It is about a totality of well-being where mind, body, will and spirit cohere in a togetherness that alone brings healing and wholeness to the whole person. In this sense, the whole work of the nation should be a *health* service, a means of enabling every person to be whole and well, and providing the support that this requires, be it in the service of physical well-being, or in education, recourse to law, mental health, financial security, and care when elderly.

These ideas for wholeness and *shalom*, cohering around a new vision for the common good, can be the way that we rebuild our nation and change its heart.

I cannot be the person who tells you exactly what this will look like. Nor can any one person. Or any one political party. Not only do I not have the necessary expertise or experience in all these areas, I know that changes like these can only be achieved by people coming together, and by a determination to re-set the compass of their lives through a re-orientation and a shared set of values. Only this can deliver the change that is needed. Diversity is important, not just because it is fair, but because by hearing every voice and every perspective we are much more likely to find the solutions that work for everyone and where no group feels excluded. Moreover, in my experience, which is the real heart of this letter, only God can make this change, because God is community and because God restores us to ourselves and to each other in Christ.

Without God, and without this expansive vision, we are much more likely to carry on putting ourselves first.

Such a new orientation of our life together must be realised at all the different levels in which we live, beginning with our immediate household and family. (We will always need corner shops as well as supermarkets.) It is in the household of our family units in all their variety that we will nurture and main-tain the values that underpin everything else. This will constantly extend outwards to our local communities and regions as well as to the nation. As we move towards regional empowerment of one sort or another these values will be particularly impor-tant. Having lived in the south of England for the past fifteen years and having spent nearly ten years in Yorkshire – and now living there again – I am keenly aware of a very real north–south divide and of the fact that London itself increasingly feels and often operates like a separate country.

We will bring ourselves back together in three ways. First, by a greater regional devolution and empowerment, so that cohesive and ambitious regions like Yorkshire can be enabled to take greater self-determining responsibility for issues that immediately affect their life, re-balancing the nation away from what often feels like London and the rest. Second, we must ensure that the principle of a United Kingdom, four countries in one nation, a fascinating Trinitarian model of nationhood in itself, is further strengthened by representatives of those regional assemblies and devolved governments having a greater say in Westminster. Third, we need some new ideas and innovative thinking that can take us to new places and a new normal. My hope is that this letter can play a part in lifting the spirit, raising expectations, and squeezing the creative juices of many different people who, together, may be able to collaborate on just such a venture of re-imagining.

We need an honest discussion with ourselves about national priorities. We then need to find ways of funding them that are not always in hock to the transient patterns of election cycles. The Health Service itself is again a good example. It is something we all cherish, so why not give it greater independence? And if money is an issue, which it certainly is after the huge costs of Covid-19, shouldn't we have a new discussion with ourselves about some of the things we spend our money on. This is what would happen in any well-run household. We would examine the budget. We would make priorities. And they would flow from a set of mutually agreed values and principles, not least the care of every member.

One huge expense in our national budget is Trident. Leaving aside for a moment whether Trident contravenes our commitments under the Nuclear Non-Proliferation Treaties we are signed up to, whatever one's views on the subject it costs eye-wateringly large amounts of money. Even some military leaders question the necessity of an expensive independent nuclear capability. They say there are better ways of securing our defence and making a difference in the peace-keeping our armed forces are often involved in across the world. A nuclear weapon isn't much use against a terrorist. And, of course, in a world where nuclear weapons are again proliferating, the risk of a terrorist or a rogue state getting one is only increasing. Peace-keeping forces need body armour, not nuclear weapons.

From a Christian point of view, nuclear weapons will always be deeply problematic. As recently as 2018 I led a debate in the General Synod of the Church of England in which we passed a motion declaring that Christians must 'work tirelessly for their elimination across the world'.[1] Many Christians are pacifists, but even those who are not recognise that a nuclear weapon, like a chemical weapon or a cluster bomb, could never be used, for it can never be proportionate or discriminate; therefore, like chemical weapons and cluster bombs, they should be banned. But even if you don't share this view, the huge expense of Trident and the great need we encounter elsewhere should, at least, make us pause and think again.

There are probably other expenditures we need to look at. Again, none of this is any longer about left or right, but about a new conversation with ourselves that is rooted in the values and principles upon which we wish to build our lives. What is not in doubt is the urgent need elsewhere.

We certainly need a benefit system that can properly serve the poor, but, as I have intimated already, simply providing a safety net is not enough. We need a living wage, and for those who simply can't work, or where no work is available, we need a benefit provision that is dignified and apposite. Other ideas, such as a Universal Basic Income (UBI), could also be explored. These things cost, but the cost of poverty and lost opportunity, and the very scary cost of a whole generation feeling disconnected from the rest of us, is higher. As Eve Poole has observed, in Finland, where they have introduced a pilot for UBI, 'the recipients were more satisfied with their lives and experienced less mental strain than the control group. They also had a more positive perception of their economic welfare.'[2] These are not small gains. They are ones that have an impact on all of us. Since one of the other main drivers of poverty is debt, a small universal income could make a big difference. It is a step towards a greater wholeness and a greater fairness.

We clearly and obviously also need a new determination to fund social care properly. But we also need to strengthen those institutions that support public life and the common good. We would all have different lists of which institutions are of the greatest value, and that is perfectly understandable. But what should unite us is the vision that these institutions are necessary and shouldn't, therefore, only be measured by their financial profitability, nor simply be governed by the market. For me, first among these would be an *idea* rather than institution. That idea, and a very British one too, is public service broadcasting. The Reithian vision of broadcasting that entertains, educates and informs is, in my view, even more relevant today in a media environment overwhelmed by choice and where fake news and the various echo chambers of extreme views increasingly dominate. In the British media ecology, public service broadcasting has tended to mean the BBC, and we should not overlook the tremendous good that the BBC has done not only in the life of our nation, but throughout the world. The World Service has been a beacon of hope in many dark places. There is also ITV and

Channel Four, and we if we do not cherish the almost unique contribution these institutions make to our national life, we will surely lose them, for there are some who want the market to answer all our questions, and if this were applied to the media, the BBC as we know it would quickly disappear. Of course, institutions like these can become lazy and complacent. Of course, they constantly need to be renewed. But reforming something is not the same as getting rid of it altogether. Since public service broadcasting will never be able to justify its existence through a bottom line on a balance sheet, then it is, like the NHS, another good example of why we must learn to cherish things because they *bring health*, not just because they make money.

Likewise, our armed forces, our police and emergency services, our scientific research establishments and universities, our schools and nurseries, our care homes and other international institutions such as the World Health Organization or the United Nations exist in the service of an idea that we will be a better world if we work together and if we recognise our common humanity and our responsibilities to each other.

This, too, is also the case with virtually every charitable institution, the Church itself being the largest.

Some will say that all these institutions should be paid for by charity and that they are not the responsibility of the state. This is a perfectly honourable view. However, what I am no longer able to maintain is that it is an argument between left and right. In 1944 it was a Tory, Quintin Hogg, who first coined the term 'social security'; today, it is Angela Merkel who summed up the challenge of the coronavirus as a 'test of our solidarity, our common sense and our love for each other'.[3]

For Christians, it is the love of God that compels us, and

the vision of God that requires us to live and work together. If there is a distinction, it is not so much between left and right, but between public and private. Are these things our responsibility collectively or individually? I believe the Christian narrative continuously pushes us towards the collective, but never at the expense of the individual. Once again we return to our doctrine of God: the God who is one God in three persons; who is individual *and* collective; who cares for the individual person, and who constantly draws us into community.

We need what I am going to call a new patriotism. This letter is, after all, addressed to 'Dear England', and although, as I have already emphasised, I want us to remain a part of a United Kingdom, and, post-Brexit, I hope we can establish really good and prosperous relationships with Europe, I am English and this letter is written primarily to the English.

As Archbishop of York, one of my titles is Primate of England. I write this letter out of my new responsibility to speak to the nation about the things of God and where they lead. This is my country, and I love it, but not only have we slipped from our Christian moorings, I fear we have also forgotten how to love ourselves. There is also a poverty of meaning. The narratives that have shaped our nation no longer serve us in the way they used to. Or else their reference point is something that has either disappeared or really needs to be left behind. I'm thinking of our colonial past and our not-always-healthy fascination with the events of the Second World War. The empire that we established in the nineteenth century and its gradual collapse in the twentieth century has left behind a mixed inheritance. Of course it achieved good things, and of course our relationship with what is now the Commonwealth is another vital and positive means whereby we can express community together across the world. But there were also atrocities and failings. They leave a legacy we have found it hard to consider. Part of that is still played out in the institutional racism of many of our organisations. We need to face this.

Second, the Blitz and Dunkirk, despite being defining moments in Europe's fight against Hitler, have also become touchstones for our own self-understanding, and we keep going back to them. It is good that out of the crisis of warfare a unifying vision was born. However, we seem to be leaving the vision behind while still re-playing the events of the war itself. Our partners in Europe sometimes look at us incredulously, as if we haven't quite allowed the Second World War ever to end. Hence some of our rhetoric about Europe over the years, especially in some newspaper headlines, drew heavily on the mythology of war and conquest, and a concept of Britishness that defined us against our neighbour.

We are an island. All that water around us makes a difference. Going abroad for us has always been an adventure. We can't do it by accident as is the case in many other countries. And we shouldn't stop being proud of the part we played in the defeat of fascism and the abominable ideas that went with it. But in constructing a new patriotism, we should focus on those ideas that are most likely to enable us to come together and build community with each other and with the other nations of the world. The ideas that came out of the Second World War, and behind them the Christian social vision that, at the time, was still able to capture the imagination of the country, need to be born again. We urgently need this, for without these narratives that draw us together, we are likely to slip further apart. As we shall see in our final chapters, the biggest challenge facing the world is not

Covid-19, but climate change. This absolutely requires international collaboration. Yet we are living through times when international collaboration feels more threatened than at any time since the Second World War.

What I'm suggesting is this: when we clapped on Thursday evenings we weren't just clapping for the NHS, nor even simply the other essential workers we had come to appreciate, we were applauding that very set of ideas that I am writing about here. We may not have made the connection between them and our Christian heritage. But we were saying something about the kind of society we wanted to live in, one where basic care, in this instance healthcare, is available to everyone. We were thanking those whose own lives were at risk in the service of these ideas.

Pulling together, teamwork, collaboration – these are the best of what it is to be human: they reflect the very being of God, and they are, therefore, the best of British. They can become a new Englishness, one that is not defined in opposition to others, but, as in the United Kingdom itself, in a new and collaborative set of relationships. I am proud to be English *and* British. And European in a newly defined way. I want to live in a society that doesn't just care about profit for its own sake, but uses wealth in the service of others, not in the service of personal gain. To achieve this we must be prepared to pool our resources and work for our families, communities, regions and nation in such a way that everyone has a fair share and an opportunity to thrive. Emblematic of this kind of nationhood are our treasured institutions: the National Health Service; public service broadcasting; schools and youth services; nurseries and care homes; maybe even the Church of England as well! And we might add libraries, youth organisations, local charities, the U3A, book clubs, allotments, ramblers' associations, football teams large and small, and all those things that bring us and bind us together, helping us to be more than ourselves in community with others.

We don't necessarily need new ideas, but we do need the ideas that have shaped the Christian faith to be confidently and humbly re-expressed so that they can again shape our national life. This could be a new Englishness shaped by the gospel of Christ – a determination not to be defined by separation and opposition.

Most of us don't like it when we see politicians slinging abuse at each other, or rival groups clashing in the streets.

We don't want to be divided by easy slogans or cheap rhetoric.

We are not this or that.

We don't think compromise is a dirty word.

We don't think changing your mind is a failure.

We rejoice in our diversity and difference.

We are united by our values, especially those of working together for the common good.

To our very great surprise, we find these values renewed by our appreciation of and participation in the life and worship of God. The values we live by flow from our belief in the God who came to us in Christ to show us this way of living and to save us from ourselves. Therefore, we will not be pushed off course by tomorrow's headline, however excoriating. We have a big vision for a different kind of nation and world. We are playing a long game.

CHAPTER SIXTEEN

It might be too simplistic to say that Covid-19 was caused by our misuse and exploitation of the natural world. But it would also be stupid to suggest there is no connection.

As well as reminding us that God wants justice, the Old Testament prophets offer a constant reminder that actions have consequences. Sometimes this is couched in the language of punishment, but consequence is a better way of looking at it: it is a punishment we bring upon ourselves by failing to see or anticipate where our actions lead.

It is generally held to be the case that Covid-19 originated in the so-called wet markets of China where wild animals are sold for human consumption: a virus that originated in animals jumped to humans.

The animals in these markets are taken from the wild. They are transported over large distances. They are crammed together in cramped cages. They are stressed and immuno-suppressed and therefore vulnerable to infections from each other. The people in the markets who are in close contact with the slaughtered animals are, therefore, exposed to novel pathogens. This, said Dominic Jermey, the Director of the Zoological Society of London, in an article entitled 'Humanity's exploitation of wildlife is putting us all at risk', is 'the ideal environment for new diseases to emerge'.[1]

In the same way that our unrelenting chopping down of forests to create grazing land for cattle is fuelled by our

seemingly insatiable desire for cheap meat, so our unwillingness to see the connection between our actions and their
consequences damages the health of the world. The pandemic
itself is not damaging the planet – in fact, it has given it a
bit of a breather – but it would be very foolish of us not to
see that it is misuse and exploitation of the natural world
that are creating the conditions whereby new diseases emerge
and spread. Our love of international travel means they
spread fast.

When the first lockdown came to an end, there was much
rejoicing when drive-through McDonald's reopened. Huge
queues were reported. I found this enormously depressing
because the reason Covid-19 came into being and the reason
the planet itself cries out in pain is so connected to the human
desire to have everything that we want when we want it, and
usually on a plate.

Forget the elimination of single-use plastics for a moment
– which if we ever did summon up the moral courage to
achieve wouldn't actually affect our lifestyles very much – for
me what is most emblematic of our unwillingness to change
our lifestyles or see the connection between our actions and
the misery of the planet is our voraciously unquenchable
appetite for cheap hamburgers.

Sometimes the queues were more than an hour long.
Customers, however, were not deterred.

The common household of the global human family
inhabits a common home: this beautiful, fragile oasis of
teeming and effervescent life. For too long we have thought
of it as belonging to us and that we can basically do with it
what we like. Now we must learn again how to be stewards.

There is not space in this letter to speak at great length
about what this means. Nevertheless, it is the single greatest

challenge we face: greater even than Covid-19. But not neces-sarily as obvious. Climate change might kill my grandchildren in years to come and after I've died. Covid-19 might kill me tomorrow.

However, in the midst of this current crisis we catch a glimpse of a different future. It is, for instance, unlikely that we will ever go back to a pattern of meeting with each other that does not, before a meeting is planned, at least consider whether it could just as easily take place via a video-conferencing facility, thus saving time and carbon. We will still meet in person, but we will come to distinguish between different types of meeting and the different ways of gathering they require. Holidays in England may seem attractive again. We may become more discerning about how frequently we travel by plane. We may continue to shop locally. We may even learn to eat less meat, for just this simple decision would have a massive impact on the health of the planet. The Monday-to-Friday working week may also change and adapt. For many of us, working at home will become the norm. We may make do and mend in the ways that previous generations took for granted. The digital world may even mature and come of age.

There are challenges here as well as opportunities. Our economy will probably have to adapt to a new status quo where city centres no longer have so many workers commuting into them. Among others, the small service businesses that have thrived around this economic model will be affected acutely. As always, the poor are in greatest danger. Their work is under most threat. They are least likely to be able to work from home. They will have limited opportunities to adapt.

But the most dangerous future of all is the one where we

just go back to how things were and carry on exhausting the planet at the same reckless rate of knots that is jeopardising its very health and future. Let me take just one example, and let it stand for so many others I could have chosen: ancient trees.

We probably all know about the colossal loss of rainforests that has gone largely unchecked in recent years, cut down for the cattle to graze so that we can have the meat we crave. Alongside this, other vast forests are lost because of drought and fire. But recent studies also show that trees in our remaining forests are dying at increasingly high rates, especially the bigger, older trees.

Even if there is no forest fire, hotter weather weakens trees. Longer dry seasons followed by torrential rain and massive floods alter the mix of trees. Certain species have been driven beyond the threshold of what they can handle. Forests are getting younger. This threatens biodiversity, eliminating important plant and animal habitats, and reducing forests' ability to store the excess carbon dioxide that is generated by our consumption of fossil fuels.

Trees are hugely important for holding and designing the ecosystems around them for other plant and animal life. Without them, the soil can quickly become desert. And, apart from swarms of insects, whose devastating arrival is on the rise in many deserts and semi-desert regions of the world, there is no life at all.

In an earlier chapter, I mentioned my association with the diocese of Marsabit in northern Kenya, where I witnessed drought and heard about flood. In my most recent correspondence with Bishop Qampicha, he told me there are now plagues of locusts, bigger and more devastating than anyone living can remember.

Trees are one of the best ways of taking carbon dioxide out of the atmosphere and storing it naturally. Trees absorb CO_2 and use it to build new materials, such as trunks, stems and roots. Therefore, in the not so recent past, there was a hope and an assumption that rising carbon dioxide levels would feed tree growth. But this has not happened. As the planet gets hotter, trees respond by shedding their leaves or closing their pores to retain moisture. Both of these reactions curtail carbon absorption. One scientist described this as like 'going to an all you can eat buffet with duct tape over your mouth'.[2]

This is making a bad situation worse. In a tropical rainforest, the vast majority of tree mass is usually in the top 1 per cent of the largest trees. This disproportionately holds the above-ground carbon storage. But they are the ones dying. This may create space for new trees, but they have much less capacity for carbon storage, and are themselves in danger as well.

I use this example of trees because when we travel by plane, many of us tick the carbon-offset box when we book. We pay a little extra to salve our conscience. What we are usually buying is trees. However, the assumption that just planting more trees will itself enable us to carry on with an unchanged lifestyle is dangerously complacent. The evidence is in the trees themselves: not just the ones we still cut down in great numbers, but those that are dying even though we planted them – especially the ones we need the most, the ancient trees planted hundreds of years ago.

Good forest management, from planting acacia trees in place of pine and cypress in the hottest parts of the world, to improving the rate at which carbon is absorbed by increasing the growth rate of the tree itself, and reducing the amount of carbon dioxide eventually returned to the atmosphere by using wood as timber rather than fuel, will all help. And of course, we still need to plant trees. This continues to be the one thing many of us can do in our own back gardens if we have one, or at least we can contribute to community and global tree-planting projects. But we have to limit our use of carbon as well. We have to fly less. We have to become less dependent upon goods and products that are flown around the world for our satisfaction. We have to transition more swiftly and more courageously to a non-carbon future. We have to be prepared to make the sacrifices that this requires. We don't need strawberries all year round. We can go to Scarborough instead of Spain. We can regenerate local industries. We can buy locally sourced food. We have to make sure that the poor do not end up footing the bill, especially the poor in the poorest parts of the world.

The habitats of the world are changing and must change again. We are closer to the brink of devastating damage than most of us are prepared to consider. But this is where we may learn again from the horrors and privations of the coronavirus pandemic. It came upon us quickly, and despite the failings and prevarications of government in the first month or so, we soon started to adapt. This adaptation has not been easy, and there have been many mistakes and much suffering along the way, but we have demonstrated to ourselves that it is possible to change and live differently. We should take heart from this, and now apply the same determination to change and adapt to this much bigger and more frighteningly existential challenge.

Once again, writing neither as a politician, nor an economist, nor a climatologist, but as a follower of Jesus, I turn to our Scriptures and traditions for resource and encouragement.

Returning to that beautiful passage from Paul's letter to the Colossians, beginning, 'He is the image of the invisible God' that I quoted way back, we can now note the astonishing assertion that just as 'in him all the fullness of God was pleased to dwell' so the peace that Christ secured through the shedding of his blood on the cross was in order to 'reconcile to himself all things, *whether on earth or in heaven*'.

Ruth Valerio makes the point that we usually limit the saving work of Christ to people. But 'Paul here is broadening out our understanding of salvation to include all things . . . the God who created the world is the same God who redeems us and his whole creation through his Son, Jesus Christ.'[3]

We spoke earlier about how Christ's death on the cross breaks barriers down. Now we can see that this embraces the whole creation.

We are inheritors of this tradition. The Scriptures require us to be stewards of the earth. The great biblical vision is that we might also work with God for the renewal of the earth that in the Bible is sometimes referred to as a new heaven and a new earth. It is about establishing God's peace, 'here on earth as it is in heaven'.

As we reach for the moral vision and the capacity for change that this endeavour asks of us, trees might help us in other ways. They have things to teach us. They are emblematic of a different way of inhabiting the world.

In 2020, Radio Four ran an occasional series on trees, inviting different people – both expert horticulturalists and, as it turned out, amateur tree lovers like me – to talk about why they loved trees. I was interviewed beside the splendid tulip tree that grows in the garden in Essex where I used to live before moving to York. I'm not quite a tree hugger, but I did confess to never being able to suppress the very human desire to touch a tree, or even, while I'm still comparatively agile, climb up into its branches to see the world from its perspective and to become part of its domain. I told the interviewer how I loved the resolute stillness of a tree, the way it accepted what it was and where it was, and the way it worked in harmonious collaboration with the grass, plants and animals around it.

For several years I've been working on a poem about trees that I can never quite figure out how to conclude. But I'm pleased with the opening line. It begins: 'You are extremely good at standing still.'

A tree is rooted – literally! – in time and space. It moves by going deeper and growing higher, not by travelling somewhere else. It is in tune with the habitat of which it is a part. It accepts things from that habitat and contributes things back in a symphonic equilibrium of giving and receiving. Trees know how to adapt. They accept the difference of each season. A tree in winter is no less healthy than a tree in spring. Provided there are nutrients in the soil, sun in the sky, water in the clouds and bees to pollinate their flowers, they know that fruitfulness comes in due season.

Trees pay attention to their roots. They know that in this way fruitfulness will take care of itself. In other words, they know how to rely on others. They receive as well as give. Their branches and their bark are home to others.

No wonder the source of life in the Garden of Eden is a tree.

We, on the other hand, are more fidgety. We find it increasingly difficult to be present. We are always looking over our shoulder. We anxiously fret about the future. We rake over the past. We have almost completely lost the ability to grow and flourish where we are, let alone seek the interior growth that comes from putting down deep roots. We want instant, year-round fruitfulness with graphs that only ever surge upwards in one direction. It works for a season. Just about. But then it kills us.

A life lived in community with God is a rooted life. It is a life of seasons. It is a life lived in inter-dependence with others. It makes us, as the very first psalm in the Bible puts it, 'like trees planted by streams of living water', yielding fruit in due season, and whose leaves do not wither.

This is a radical change. It is the life lived with God that this book seeks to commend. But even the word 'radical', let us remember, comes from the Latin word *radix*, meaning root. It is about a return. It is about getting back to the root of a thing. In this case the very root of our humanity as those who are made in the image of God and charged to be stewards of God's creation and destined, here and now and in what is to come, to live our lives in community with God. Nothing else has that same power to change us and change the world.

It is God who will save us. It is God who will transform us. The cross of his Son, Jesus Christ, is the tree of life. From the barren emptiness of what seemed like hopeless and empty defeat, flowers are blossoming.

CHAPTER SEVENTEEN

Most of my school reports included a line somewhere saying that I was a bit of a dreamer.

I am guilty as charged. I spent a lot of my schooldays staring out of the window, dreaming. Adult life hasn't much changed me, though on the whole I am better at hiding it when necessary.

If you have got this far in the book, you may well be a fellow sufferer.

The Bible is also full of dreamers. Youngest children, exiles and outcasts who long for a different world are always being pulled into the centre of the story. Abraham looks up into a star-filled sky and sees his own future. Joseph, the husband of Mary, closes his ears to the sensible wisdom of those who advise him to wash his hands of his young fiancée and puts his faith in a dream instead.

My dream is that in living our lives in communion with God we may find the peace we crave.

Like God, we are distinct and individual. The universe is not a part of God. It has its own separate life, as God does. And so do we. Each of us is a separate creation. We all have a deep sense of self, a deep desire to make the best of life, and an inbuilt longing to find meaning, purpose and value for our lives. But, like God, we are also communal. We belong to each other and are responsible to each other. We find ourselves in relation to each other and to

God. Once we realise this, everything changes, starting with us.

Like God, we are creative, wanting to love and receive love, to shape and understand our lives and our environment, to better ourselves, and to live life to the full.

However, through fear and failing and because the drive to self-preservation sometimes leads us to forget that the best way of preserving self is to lose it and seek a greater, common good, we turn in on ourselves. We start to understand ourselves not in relationship to others but over and against them.

Therefore, the first and most dangerous sin of all, the author of every other sin, is the enthroning of self and the denial of community. We worship an idol. We exchange the real fulfilment that life has to offer through living in community for a hedonistic pursuit of transient self-centred and self-obsessed pleasure. It is this worldview that leads to the spiteful gossip, casual bullying, unchecked unkindness and carefully crafted cynicism of so much daily life and then, inexorably, from one degree of loathing to another, to the pillaging of the world itself, its natural resources seen as my possession; to then, the exploitation of the poor and the demonising of the outcast and, beyond that point, to where I am so at the centre that I can no longer even see the humanity of those who are my neighbour, to race hatred, and the pogroms of ethnic cleansing. This is the way it goes. We always stand at the brink of disaster and we can always choose which way to go. If you don't think this describes you, then you are probably most in danger. This is often demonstrated in that most innocent of remarks when, seeing the latest horror on the news, we say, 'I can't imagine what makes people act like this.' In the twinkling of an eye, we reveal our imagined superiority and claim immunity from even the possibility that we inhabit the same flesh and are capable of the same outrages that others commit. By reckoning them less than human we pave the way for the next holocaust. Or else we just cover things up, thinking that our own estimation of our own goodness (despite the evidence to the contrary) is enough, and we will never have to be accountable for our mistakes. We build walls around ourselves. We build walls around our families, our communities, our nations. We call it security. But it is usually fear. It can quickly become hatred. We found out long ago that attack is the best form of defence. We need to learn another way: the way of Christ.

Furthermore, these are not things we 'progress' away from. As Camus writes in the final sentence of his great novel *The Plague* (required reading in 2020!), the virus that had caused such misery and death – be it the deadly rat-carried bacillus that overwhelmed the city of Oran where the novel is set, the Covid-19 that reaches across the world in our breath and our contact with each other or the just-as-deadly soul-denying ideologies of fascism that are actually the main subject of the book – 'never dies or vanishes entirely . . . it can remain dormant for years in furniture or clothing . . . it waits patiently in bedrooms, cellars, trunks, handkerchiefs and old papers . . . and perhaps the day will come when, for the instruction or misfortune of mankind, the plague will rouse its rats and send them to die in some well-contented city'.[1]

The deeper and less palatable truth is that we are all capable of the most magnificent and selfless loving, and all capable of the most appalling horror. And God won't stop us or control us. God won't intervene when we abuse and exploit and kill. God will not force our hands or hearts to love. Not because God doesn't want to, and not because God doesn't care, and not because God is not able, but because that is the nature of love. If God intervened at this level with our freedom, we would become incapable of love, we would be something other than human: just a much-loved pet, not a child or heir. Which does not mean God cannot help, only that we first need to make a connection between those spiritual longings inside us and the origin of life, which is the self-giving love of God. Then, when we are in tune with God, we can ourselves be the answer to our prayers and begin to make a difference in the world.

This is how we will find fulfilment. This is where we will learn to be ourselves – by entering into right relationship with others and, through God, with life itself. This is where the help on offer will be guidance on how to live life well: a compass, not a map. This is where the promise is an abundant life: not a life purged of pain, but an invitation to collaborate with God in building a different sort of world altogether. Just as we always stand on the brink of disaster, the disaster that comes from our own wrong choices and their terrible consequences, we also stand before a God who endlessly loves us and endlessly holds out the possibility of change.

And, of course, in every life, and certainly in every Christian life, there is darkness and difficulty. Sometimes the darkness seems overwhelming. But the God who shares our life in Christ is the God of darkness *and* light. In every moment, in the darkest hour, and in the eye of every storm, we have the opportunity to repent, to turn around, to receive this chance to start again and change direction. We also know that we are held: held in the darkness and carried into the light.

It is never too late for love. We can never be so lost that God cannot find us, never so lonely that God will not embrace and befriend us, never so locked in that God cannot break through. It is never so dark that the radiance of Christ cannot illuminate the way, though sometimes the light seems very faint indeed.

We call this a new life, but it is sensible to remember that it is not a different life. It is this life, the life we have in this one world, but richer and more precious, and shot through with a purpose beyond the satisfaction of self. It is a true finding of self in relation to others: what Jesus calls losing your life in order to find it.

Its effects are revolutionary. Knowing that we are loved and accepted by God, we start to love each other. We start looking out for each other. We take the fragile brilliance of the one small light we see and kindle others from it. Our capacity for love and generosity is increased. We are able to be merciful to others because we have come to be realistic about the mercy we need ourselves. This kind of generous, humble, merciful loving flows out of us. It hungers and thirsts for justice. It dreams of peace. In fact, in the end, Jesus says that love will be the great authenticating mark of those who follow him.

On the night before he dies, gathered with his closest friends and having just washed their feet, Jesus says these words: 'I give you a new commandment, that you love one another. Just as I have loved you, you also should love one another. By this everyone will know that you are my disciples, if you have love for one another.'[2]

Sadly, we don't always see this love in the lives of his followers today. But when we do, it is something refreshingly beautiful and somehow easily recognisable. Goodness is very attractive. Love is the language we can all speak, even if we've never encountered it much before. We hear love's voice, or simply see love in action, and we are drawn to it, inspired by it, changed by it, and even start loving ourselves. Some people's lives have been so damaged and so abused that this will take time. Love will have to burrow through deep defences of hurt and resentment, outpourings of bitterness and anger, even violence, but love will win.

Neither is it too fanciful to see that it is this self-forgetful love, the love that we see in Christ and that we are called to embody, that is the main reason the Christian faith has triumphed. It triumphed against the brutal persecutions of the past. It can triumph over the apathy, hedonism, careless-ness and self-absorbed indifference of today. But only by loving. Only a simpler, more humble, more loving Church can be the Church of Jesus Christ.

Let me give you one last very famous example from the past. You probably know that Constantine was the first Christian emperor of Rome, though how much of a Christian he was himself is another matter. To keep power he had most of his family murdered!

His nephew, Julian, became emperor after him, and though he was raised in a Christian family, his education was steeped in Greek philosophy. He loved the writings of Aristotle and Plato on the subject of the virtuous life. Therefore, when he became emperor he announced that he was a follower of 'Hellenism', the old Greek religion of Zeus and Athena and innumerable other deities, and he set about trying to stamp out Christianity. But it was too late. Christianity would not go away.

Why is the Church so successful among the masses? he asked himself. It couldn't be Christian doctrine, he thought, for he was convinced that his own philosophical arguments had disproved Christianity conclusively. So it had to be the way Christians actually lived their lives.

Consequently, in his capacity as 'pope' of the new paganism, Julian wrote a letter to his head priest in Galatia, ordering him to make sure that the pagan priests acted more like Christians. Julian was very specific: 'Christians have charity, and we don't . . . we need to imitate them if we're going to compete with them.'[3] And the final nonsensical evidence for this was famously expressed when he noted that the Christians he encountered didn't just relieve their own poor, they 'relieve ours as well!'

This was the reason the Christian faith had triumphed. It was love. Loving enemies as well as loving your own.

But Julian failed. He was killed in battle, and a legend has it that as he fell from his horse his last words were, 'You win, Galilean.'

Centuries later, another Julian, an English anchorite nun and mystic who was very close to death, received a series of revelations of God's love, and wrote this at the end of her book as a summing up of all that she had learned from looking on the passion of Christ: 'Love was his meaning.'[4] The whole meaning of the Christian life, the Christian response, and the Christian vocation summed up in a single word: love.

But, as we know, love isn't easy. It doesn't always come naturally, and if loving even those who are close to us is hard, how much harder is it to follow the way of Christ and love our enemies as well, to offer those who smite us the other cheek, to share our possessions and our wealth and to walk the second mile of love.

The new direction of the Christian life doesn't just mean turning away from what is self-seeking and destructive, it means embracing the way of Christ, the true hope of the world.

In Jesus we see what perfect love looks like, the love that lays down its life for its friends. In the Gospels Jesus says that if you want to be his follower you must take up your cross too.[5] You must share in God's suffering and redemptive love for all the world. This is a dream worth following, a life worth living.

Just as I was finishing this book, literally writing this last chapter, I received a letter from another dreamer like me, a retired priest in the Chelmsford diocese sharing with me his reflections on the world that we might reconstruct as we start to recover and move out of the world of Covid-19. It was another example of how the Christian vision shapes life. And that there is nothing new under the sun. Especially human forgetfulness. He reminded me of the papal encyclical *Rerum Novarum*, which was published by Pope Leo XIII in 1891 and that laid the foundations for Roman Catholic social teaching and for the justice and peace movement. Its principles include: the dignity of labour; the universal distribution of goods, reminding us that our possessions are not really our own, but gifts from God; gratuity – that is, recognising God's abundant generosity to us and the challenge for us to be similarly generous to others; the common good – that is, the concern that everyone in the human household flourishes; solidarity, reminding us that we belong to one another irrespective of ethnicity, language, religion, education or status; and subsidiarity. All of these were a great encouragement that this dream of a better world is worth pursuing and its principles are the principles of God's kingdom.

At about the same time that *Rerum Novarum* was published, Charles Peguy, a noted French poet and essayist, a believing but non-practising Roman Catholic, wrote a number of poems that were either imagined conversations with God or sometimes entitled 'God's dream'.

Despite having a couple of volumes of his work, I have been unable to source this particular poem. I just have it on a photocopied sheet of paper that someone gave me at a training seminar at least twenty years ago, but it resonates with my own dream for a Church that, based upon these principles, dreams of inhabiting the world differently, and could even end up changing the world, enabling us to find the peace that is God's great desire for his people and his world. It feels like a good place to end:

I myself will dream a dream within you –
    Good dreams come from me, you know –
My dreams seem impossible,
    not too practical,
    not for the cautious man or woman –
        a little risky sometimes,
        a trifle brash perhaps –
Some of my friends prefer
    to rest more comfortably,
        in sound asleep,
        with visionless eyes –
But, from those who share my dreams
    I ask a little patience,
        a little humour,
        some small courage,
        and listening heart –
I will do the rest –

Then they will risk
    and wonder at their daring –

Dear England

Run – and marvel at this speed –
Build – and stand in awe at the beauty of their
   building –

You will meet me often as you work –
     in your companions, who share the risk
     in your friends, who believe in you enough
        to lend their own dreams
        their own hands
        their own hearts
          to your building –
In the people who will stand in your doorway,
    stay awhile,
        and walk away knowing that they, too,
           can find a dream.

There will be sun-filled days,
    and sometimes it will rain –
       a little variety –
       both come from me.

So come now, be content
It is my dream you dream –
   my house you build –
my caring you witness –
my love you share,
and this is the heart of the matter.

POSTSCRIPT

Having thoroughly unpacked the things I said to that young woman at Paddington Station, as this letter finishes let me return briefly to the powerful and insightful things she said to me. She spoke about people of faith either inhabiting their faith as if it were a hobby, or else holding on to it so tightly that others were frightened away.

Sadly, both these tendencies are not difficult to find. There are people who seem perfectly capable of sitting in church week by week and year by year and hearing the astonishing challenge and beauty of the Christian message but not in any way allowing it to affect the life they lead. And I don't just mean that cultural blindness where in every generation our own presuppositions and assumptions easily prevent us from seeing what to future generations will appear obvious (like our response to slavery), but the impossible-to-ignore or argue-away obviousness of loving your neighbour and of giving to the poor.

Or there are people, like me I suppose, who are excited and inspired by the message, but are better at talking about it than living it out. Like the medieval knights who, when they were baptised, held their right arms – the ones that held their swords – out of the baptismal waters; so it is all too easy to put one's Christian faith in a box marked 'Sunday', but leave the other days of the week in one's own possession. We know what we should do; we know what lives we should be leading; but we never get round to making the changes that are required. We'll do it tomorrow.

The fanaticism that young woman alludes to is also horribly prevalent. There is no bigot quite like a religious bigot. Which is why I've tried to tell this story by describing myself as a follower of Jesus rather than a follower of religion. The more one becomes embedded in the life of a religious institution the harder this gets (don't I know it!). Defending the institution becomes the all-consuming preoccupation. This has led to many ills. But the fanatical and obsessive conviction that I am not just right, but must stamp out anything and anyone who disagrees with me, is even more frightening. Such zealous clarity doesn't only exist in the religious mind. Secular totalitarian philosophies have been equally successful in breeding hatred. However, for both, looking and learning from Jesus is the best cure available. He leads us to God, who is community and who delights in diversity. He asks us to love our enemies and he shows us what this looks like. He demonstrates the cost.

'Is there another way?' she asked me. Well, that is what this letter has been about. Addressed to England, it tries to steer a loving path between complacency and extremism. Indeed, such moderation and provisionality may itself be quite an English thing.

What I wanted to do on Paddington Station was not try and persuade her to see things in the same way as me. I wasn't, in that sense, trying to convert her. But neither did I want to sell her short by pretending these things don't matter, or that they are just a question of personal choice or leisure-time pursuit.

These things do matter. If what I'm saying is true, it is the most important truth of all and, as I said earlier, the truth upon which all other truths, and all love and all goodness, are contingent. In this sense I *did* want to convert her, not by selling her some sort of sordid spiritual time-share in a fluffy and rose-tinted pretence of heaven, but enabling her to see the truth about God more clearly and then decide for herself what to do next. I wanted to show her Jesus. Because he is the best cure. He is the one who shows us what our humanity is supposed to be like. Just showing her myself would never be enough. Like everyone else, I am too much a work in progress and not yet the saint I am called to be, whose transparency of life could enable others to see Jesus in me as if he were standing before them.

Hopefully, she caught a glimpse. But that would be as much through good listening and the gift of time as through anything I said. And, as we know, time is constrained.

What I could do in the few moments we had was say what I said and then point her in the direction of a local church, praying and hoping that she would find there other seekers after the way of life. And, of course, I don't know what happened next for her.

But what I would have liked is a longer conversation. And, being English, and if the circumstances were different, I would have probably suggested we put the kettle on and settle down for a chat over a cup of tea.

Funnily enough, if she did ever make it to church, this is what she would have discovered. A bunch of men and women gathered around a table, conversing with each other and with God, and finding a way for life. The staple diet of the Church's worship is a service called the Eucharist – a Greek word meaning thanksgiving. It's what you will very likely find – or something like it – if you decide to give the community of the Church a chance.

Remembering the meal that Jesus shared on the night before he died, Christian people break bread and pour wine. We see in this action the lived-out parable of Jesus' dying and rising. We receive, in bread and wine, the iron rations of life with God. Sometimes this service is called Holy Communion. This emphasises that belonging to God and belonging to each other is itself the radical Christian message. Sometimes it is just called Mass, the final Latin word from the Roman Catholic order of the service. It means 'go'. Go out into the world and live another way. Go out into the world and share what you have received. Go out into the world and make a difference.

That young woman's questions and our little conversation changed and goes on changing me; the refining fire of her questions has helped me to think again about and learn afresh how to be a follower of Jesus.

My main hope for her is that she goes on. How could it be anything else? For that is God's hope for each of us. God made us and loves us and will go on with that love for us however we choose to respond.

I hope that you may be changed by this letter and I hope our nation and our world may be changed as well.

But only you can make that change. God won't do it for you. Love does not insist on its own way.[6] But God will wait. Then, when you respond to God, go out into that bit of the world that is your life and your domain and be the difference you long to see.

Centuries ago, the prophet Ezekiel encouraged the people of Israel by telling them how God was going to restore their fortunes and bring them back to their own land. In this beautiful passage, God promises to sprinkle them with clean water and give them a new heart. But not a heart of stone, a heart of flesh[7]; not a super-bionic 'never to be broken again' heart, but a heart like Jesus': one that is able to feel the biting sorrow of the world and one that can enter into its joys; a heart that can laugh and cry; a heart that will beat in time to the rhythm of God. Then, when our hearts are changed, when God puts God's heart in us, the world will be changed as well.

Dear England, let us go in peace.

Let us take heart.

ACKNOWLEDGEMENTS

From one small conversation a whole book has grown. It is a conversation I have thought about a lot and spoken about a lot, so as I consider who to thank for the making of this book, I have to start with that young woman on Paddington Station. I never found out her name, and I very much doubt whether we will ever meet again, but I do entertain a small hope that somehow this book might find a way into her hands and she could see how her questions and her boldness in approaching me in the first place have given birth to something that I hope will help many people consider the claims of the Christian faith.

As I've written I've also thought about all the other people I know and love who do not see the beauty of Christ in the way I do. Maybe this book will help them understand my faith a bit more. It might also help them see faith differently and come to know Christ themselves.

Most of this book was written in Essex before I moved to York, and some of it at my mum's house where I often used to escape to get some writing done away from other voices and concerns. I'm grateful to my staff at Bishopscourt in Essex and Bishopthorpe here in York for helping me manage my time and encouraging me to find time to write. Matthew Simpkins read a few of the chapters and offered insightful advice, challenging and refining some of my less well considered theological pronouncements. And I'm particularly grateful to Katherine Venn and the team at Hodder for their encouragement, wisdom and critical friendship. Their input has helped the book be the best that it can be.

NOTES

Prelims
1. R.S. Thomas, 'Praise', in *Collected Poems*, Phoenix, 1993, p. 318. Used with permission.

Chapter Six
1. Genesis 1:26.
2. Hugh Montefiore, 'God Acting in Creation: The God Who Acts', Lecture given to Southwark Diocesan Conference, 1985, p. 16.
3. Quoted in Montefiore, op. cit., p. 17.
4. Song of Songs 8:7.

Chapter Seven
1. The most famous examples are probably Anselm from the eleventh century and Julian of Norwich from the fourteenth.
2. Mark 12:29–31.

Chapter Eight
1. Luke 1:26–8.
2. Colossians 1:15.
3. Colossians 1:19.

Chapter Nine
1. Acts 19:10.
2. *The Epistle to Diognetus*, Manchester University Press, 1949, pp. 79–81.
3. *The Martyrdom of Polycarp*, in *Early Christian Writings*, tr. Maxwell Staniforth, with revised translation, introductions and notes by Andrew Louth, Penguin Books, 1987, p. 127.

4. Ibid., p. 128.
5. Ibid., p. 132.
6. Acts 2:22–4, 36. This is Peter preaching the Church's very first sermon on the streets of Jerusalem on the day of Pentecost after the disciples have received the Holy Spirit. He tells people about the resurrection of Jesus and the outpouring of God's Spirit.

Chapter Ten
1. You can read the whole of this story for yourself – it isn't very long – at Luke 10:25–37.
2. Matthew 22:37–40.
3. Bernard of Clairvaux: https://www.soulshepherding.org/bernard-of-clairvauxs-four-degrees-of-love/ [accessed 7 May 2020].

Chapter Eleven
1. Matthew 5:38–45.
2. Matthew 5:48.
3. Matthew 5:3–10.
4. Romans 5:8.

Chapter Twelve
1. Galatians 3:26–9.
2. At this point in the book I must acknowledge my debt to Matthew Simpkins for his powerful and liberating exegesis of Galatians 3.28, in his MA thesis 'What should Galatians 3:28 contribute to gender ethics?'

Chapter Thirteen
1. Graham Tomlin, https://www.prospectmagazine.co.uk/philosophy/how-coronavirus-is-giving-us-a-crash-course-in-a-different-moral-universe [accessed 26 May 2020].
2. https://www.ons.gov.uk/peoplepopulationandcommunity/birthsdeathsandmarriages/families/bulletins/familiesandhouseholds/2017 [accessed 27 May 2020].
3. Karl Barth, quoted in Richard Harries, *Praying the Eucharist*, SPCK, 2004, p. 42.

Notes

Chapter Fourteen

1. I am indebted to John Dominic Crossan, who makes this point in his book, *The Greatest Prayer: Rediscovering the Revolutionary Message of the Lord's Prayer*, HarperCollins, 2010, p. 40.
2. Amos 5:21–4.
3. Isaiah 1:13–17.
4. Psalm 89:14.
5. Psalm 99:4.
6. See Micah 6:8.
7. Leviticus 23:22.
8. Exodus 23:11.
9. Leviticus 25:23.
10. See Acts 2:44.
11. https://www.theguardian.com/news/2019/dec/05/gap-between-rich-and-poor-grows-alongside-rise-in-uks-total-wealth [accessed 16 June 2020].
12. https://www.childrenssociety.org.uk/what-we-do/our-work/ending-child-poverty/what-is-child-poverty#:~:text=Four%20 million.,least%20one%20parent%20in%20work [accessed 16 June 2020].
13. Quoted in Peter C. Baker, 'We Can't Go Back to Normal', https://www.theguardian.com/world/2020/mar/31/how-will-the-world-emerge-from-the-coronavirus-crisis [accessed 3 April 2020].
14. See Shoshana Zuboff, *The Age of Surveillance Capitalism: The Fight for a Human Future at the New Frontier of Power*, Profile Books, 2019.

Chapter Fifteen

1. General Synod of the Church England, 7 July 2018.
2. Eve Poole, 'A Year of Universal Income', http://evepoole.com/a-year-of-universal-basic-income/ [accessed 4 June 2020].
3. Quoted in Neal Lawson, 'Coronavirus shows us the folly of stripping state and society to the bone', https://www.theguardian.com/commentisfree/2020/mar/19/coronavirus-stripping-state-society [accessed 17 June 2020].

Chapter Sixteen
1. Quoted in John C. Lennox, *Where is God in a Coronavirus World?*, The Good Book Company, 2020, p. 16.
2. Quoted in Craig Welch, https://www.nationalgeographic.com/science/2020/05/grand-old-trees-are-dying-leaving-forests-younger-shorter/ [accessed 5 July 2020].
3. Ruth Valerio, *Saying Yes to Life*, SPCK, 2020, p. 5.

Chapter Seventeen
1. Albert Camus, *The Plague*, Penguin Classics, 2002, pp. 237–8.
2. John 13:34–5.
3. Julian, quoted in Victor Duruy, *History of Rome and the Roman People*, Dana Estes and Charles E. Lauriat, 1887, Volume VIII, p. 175.
4. Julian of Norwich, *Revelations of Divine Love*, tr. Clifton Walters, Penguin Classics, 1966, p. 211.
5. Luke 9:23.
6. 1 Corinthians 13:5.
7. See Ezekiel 36:24–6.